TROJANS, WORMS, AND SPYWARE

TROJANS, WORMS, AND SPYWARE
A Computer Security Professional's Guide to Malicious Code

Michael Erbschloe

ELSEVIER
BUTTERWORTH
HEINEMANN

AMSTERDAM • BOSTON • HEIDELBERG • LONDON
NEW YORK • OXFORD • PARIS • SAN DIEGO
SAN FRANCISCO • SINGAPORE • SYDNEY • TOKYO

Elsevier Butterworth–Heinemann
200 Wheeler Road, Burlington, MA 01803, USA
Linacre House, Jordan Hill, Oxford OX2 8DP, UK

∞ Recognizing the importance of preserving what has been written, Elsevier prints its books on acid-free paper whenever possible.

Library of Congress Cataloging-in-Publication Data
Application submitted.

British Library Cataloging-in-Publication Data
A catalogue record for this book is available from the British Library.

ISBN: 978-0-75067-848-3

For information on all Butterworth–Heinemann publications
visit our website at http://books.elsevier.com/security

To my mother

To my friends Blaster and Razer

Table of Contents

Preface

Malicious code attacks cost businesses billions of dollars each year. Most organizations that have been hit by a malicious code attack find that response, cleanup, and restoration of computers and files is time consuming and costly. In some cases, it can take days to recover from an attack and get operations back to a normal state. It also costs money, lots of money. Three distinct sets of experience occur when an organization suffers a malicious code attack: that of the IT staff, computer users, and organization managers.

The IT staff often expends considerable effort to track down the malicious code, eliminate it, patch systems, restore files, and deal with anxious computer users and their managers, who need systems back as soon as possible. This can be frustrating and tiring work that requires long hours of unpaid overtime. This is really not the best thing for mental health, family life, or personal relationships.

Computer users have their work disrupted, files lost, and e-mail abilities crippled. They can also end up with IT staff moving around their offices examining and working to restore computers. In some cases, computer users' coworkers or associates and contacts in other organizations are spammed or hit by worms originating from their computers. This does not contribute to a pleasant work environment, and being the purveyor of a malicious code attack, even when unintended, is not a good way to make friends or get invited to lunch.

Managers have their own unique way of suffering. Productivity in work groups and in entire organizations can plummet for days at a time when computer systems and e-mail are rendered unusable. Deadlines can be missed. Customer support can fall into disarray. Perhaps worst of all, momentum can be lost. If you have been a manager and have worked to get an organization on track and everybody moving in the same direction at the same time, you know that this is not always as easy as the management gurus make it out to be. Then boom! The malicious code attack brings things to a crawl.

Computer security professionals struggle every day to develop new and improved methods of defending computer networks and systems. As computer security practices improve, defenses against the attacks become more effective. However, malicious code writers are constantly finding new ways to exploit old vulnerabilities, and they also take advantage of newly found or created vulnerabilities.

In years past, malicious code writers have been painted predominantly as socially alienated computer nerds who hacked for recreation—both to rebel against the establishment and to accomplish and brag about new feats of system intrusion into high-security corporate and government sites. But now many malicious code writers are spammers who use captured machines to launch e-mail campaigns. Others are organized crime groups from Eastern Europe who enslave machines to launch denial-of-service attacks on the systems of organizations that refuse to pay extortion money. Then there are the identity theft gangs that steal usernames, passwords, and financial account information on a for-profit basis.

In the future, things will be worse. It is widely believed that we are on the verge of a new kind of conflict known as information warfare. The terrorists and soldiers of the future are expected to attack critical infrastructures to disrupt financial services and corporate as well as government operations. Malicious code will be one of the most lethal weapons in the arsenal of cyberfighters. The computer systems and networks of your organization—and even your home computer—could easily end up being road kill in the 21st-century cyberwars.

The purpose of this book is to show organizations how to effectively and efficiently organize and maintain their defenses against malicious code attacks. The book provides background information on malicious code attacks and guidance on how to staff the malicious code defense efforts, devise methods of defense, select products to help in the defense, and train computer users to be the first line of defense in the battle against malicious code attacks.

Introduction

One of the biggest headaches that comes along with networked and Internet-connected computers is the absolute requirement of dealing with malicious code attacks. There is no choice; if your systems are not equipped in some way with antivirus protection, sooner or later some bug will eat them. There is also very little to be gained by whining about how vulnerable computer systems are to malicious code attacks. The unfortunate circumstances that wired societies face can be depicted in the following manner:

- Organizations and individuals want computing and communications resources, and they want them as cheaply as possible.

- Software and hardware manufacturers work synergistically to meet market demands for cheap but highly functional computing and communications resources.

- The corporate interests that drive cooperation between software and hardware manufacturers have resulted in a marketplace that is dominated by very few companies.

- Market dominance by very few companies has created a computing and communications technology ecology with very few species.

- The antithesis to the social forces that drive the dominant companies to cooperate in controlling the marketplace is a counterculture of malicious code writers that revels in embarrassing the corporate giants on their lack of technology prowess.

- The small number of species in the technology ecology makes it easy for the malicious code writers to find vulnerabilities and launch attacks that can spread around the world in a very short time.

Law enforcement agencies and the corporate giants that dominate the computer marketplace label malicious code writers and attackers as criminals and at times even as terrorists. The malicious code writers and attackers view the corporate giants as criminal and parasitic organizations dominated by greedy capitalists. Meanwhile, the governments of the computer-dependent parts of the world are struggling to unify their efforts to fight malicious code attacks and doing so largely under the umbrella of the global war on terrorism.

These circumstances, in the grandest of capitalistic glory, have created a marketplace in which virus protection and computer security product companies have thrived. This labyrinth of social, political, and economic forces have several results, many of which are very embarrassing for modern societies:

- Very few malicious code attackers are ever caught by the police.

- Government agencies cannot catch up with malicious code attackers, let alone build a national defense system to stop attacks.

- Large organizations that purchase technology are the prisoners of the dominant technology companies and have little recourse or market alternatives.

- Elected public officials, many of whom are the recipients of campaign contributions from the dominant technology companies, are strongly resisting confronting the industry about product liability.

When all is said and done, the burden caused by these collective and converging trends falls on you, the computer user. State and local law enforcement can do little to help in the computer security and computer crimes realm. The government, through laws and incident response by federal agencies, is often slow to react to trends. Perhaps most worrisome of all, the dominant technology companies from which you buy products—in designing the products on ever-shorter production and release cycles—do little to protect the end user. If you want to keep your computers up and running and keep the malicious code attackers at bay, you need to do two things: (1) take a comprehensive approach to dealing with malicious code attacks, and (2) become a customer of one of the well-established virus protection companies and buy, install, and maintain their products on your computer systems.

INSIDE THIS BOOK

The purpose of this book is to show organizations how to effectively and efficiently organize and maintain their defenses against malicious code attacks. Chapter 1 provides an overview of malicious code and explains the basic principles of how malicious code works and why attacks can be so dangerous for an organization. This includes an analysis of why malicious code works so well. Present and expected weaknesses in commercial off-the-shelf software are covered, as well as the many things computer users do wrong when confronted with unknown or unexpected situations.

Chapter 2 analyzes the many types of malicious code, including e-mail viruses, Trojans, worms, blended threats, and time bombs. The newest types of malicious code are also covered, including spyware, adware, and stealware. Chapter 3 provides an in-depth review of malicious code incidents that have occurred over the last decade. These include Explore.zip, Melissa, I Love You (aka Love Bug), the two variants of Code Red, SirCam, Nimda, and Slammer. The August 2003 barrage of attacks of Blaster, Qhosts, Swen.A, Sobig.F, and Welchia, and the early 2004 onslaught of multiple variants of Bagel, Netskys, MyDooms, and Hilton are also addressed.

Chapter 4 covers the basic steps organizations need to take in order to combat malicious code attacks. Analysis of the risks organizations face is provided. Guidance on how to use security policies to set standards for computing practices is provided, followed by step-by-step methods of implementing security practices, including how to manage system and patch updates. The process of how to establish a computer incident response team is covered, as well as what types of training are needed for IT professionals and end users. The chapter also provides insight into applying social engineering methods in an organization to beat back malicious code attackers, as well as how to work with law enforcement agencies.

Chapter 5 explains how to organize computer security, attack prevention, and incident response. This organization of the IT security function is covered, including where malicious code prevention fits into the IT security function and how to staff for malicious code attack prevention. The chapter also covers budgeting for malicious code attack prevention, how to establish and use alert and reporting systems, and how to evaluate products for attack prevention.

Chapter 6 focuses on how to control the computer behavior of employees. This includes a very important overview of policies on appropriate use of corporate systems and the ins and outs of monitoring employee behavior. Useful tools to control behavior are covered, including site blockers and Internet filters, content filters, chat filters, and cookie blockers. Some of the latest tools in the malicious code attack fight are also covered, including pop-up blockers, SPAM control, e-mail scanning and monitoring tools, and products that help control downloads.

Chapter 7 is a guide to responding to a malicious code incident. Topics covered include the process of establishing a first report, confirming an incident, and mobilizing a response team. This is followed by management notification procedures and using an alert system in an organization. The steps required to control and capture malicious code, identifying the source of the malicious code, the preservation of evidence, and when to call law enforcement are also covered. There is also an explanation of enterprise-wide eradication processes and how to return to normal operations.

Chapter 8 provides a model training program for end users. This includes providing basic information about malicious code, how to identify potentially malicious code, what to do if there is suspect code, and what to expect from the IT department. The model training plan also includes an explanation of how the internal warning system works and what to do if the organization is placed on alert.

Chapter 9 covers the future of malicious code attacks and defenses. This includes military-style information warfare, open-source information warfare, and militancy and social action. Homeland security efforts and international cooperation in fighting computer crimes are also covered.

At the end of each chapter, action steps that organizations can take to combat malicious code attacks are presented. These action steps turn the analysis and explanations included in each chapter into tactics and strategies that can help an organization mitigate the impact of malicious code attacks. Implementation of these action steps can help reduce the economic impact of malicious code attacks and preserve valuable resources for more constructive purposes.

Acknowledgements

I would like to acknowledge all of the staff at Butterworth–Heinemann, who worked hard to make this book possible. I appreciate all of their efforts.

My friends and companions, Brandon L. Harris and Tonya Heartfield, gave great advice and feedback on the concepts and content of this book. As always, I acknowledge the ongoing support and friendship of John Vacca. I also acknowledge the work of my editorial assistant, Kayla Lesser, who helped keep the work focused.

Michael Erbschloe

1
Malicious Code Overview

The United States Federal Bureau of Investigation (FBI), other law enforcement organizations, and security experts around the world have observed that the threat to computer systems and networks is rapidly increasing. In addition, the number and types of individuals who pose a threat have also increased, and the skill level required to attack systems has declined.

In the past, malicious code writers were predominantly viewed as socially alienated geeks who liked to have some sort of sense of accomplishment. But now many malicious code writers are spammers who use captured machines to launch e-mail campaigns. Others are organized crime groups from Eastern Europe that enslave machines to launch denial-of-service attacks on the systems of organizations that refuse to pay extortion money. Then there are the identity theft gangs that steal usernames, passwords, and financial account information on a for-profit basis.

Attackers can use a variety of off-the-shelf tools to penetrate or disrupt systems. Malicious code is simply one of their everyday tools. The FBI attributes the increase in hacking events and malicious code attacks to several sources, including the following:

- *Criminal groups*, which have increased the use of cyberintrusions for purposes of monetary gain

- *Foreign intelligence services*, which use cybertools as part of their information-gathering and espionage activities

- *Hackers*, who break into networks for the thrill of the challenge or for bragging rights in the hacker community. This activity once required a fair amount of skill or computer knowledge, but individuals can now download easy-to-use attack scripts and protocols from the Internet and launch them against victim sites.

- *Hacktivists*, who launch politically motivated attacks on publicly accessible Web pages or e-mail servers

- *Information warfare specialists*, who are supported by several nations that are aggressively working to develop information warfare doctrine, programs, and capabilities

- *Insiders*, who are disgruntled and who have become a principal source of computer crimes because their knowledge of a victim system often allows them to gain unrestricted access to cause damage to the system or to steal system data

- *Malicious code writers*, who are posing an increasingly serious threat

The United States has been approaching cybersecurity from several directions. The FBI has established computer forensics laboratories and is hiring many more agents with computer knowledge and skills. The Department of Homeland Security (DHS) was formed as a result of the terrorist attacks of September 11, 2001. Among the many responsibilities of the DHS is to implement *The National Strategy to Secure Cyberspace*, which was officially released in February 2003. It provides a framework for protecting technology assets from malicious attacks. The documents set forth the following priorities:

- Priority I: Establish a national cyberspace security response system.

- Priority II: Establish a national cyberspace security threat and vulnerability reduction program.

- Priority III: Establish a national cyberspace security awareness and training program.

- Priority IV: Secure governments' cyberspace.

- Priority V: Foster national security and international cyberspace security cooperation.

The National Strategy to Secure Cyberspace recognizes that the private sector is best equipped and structured to respond to an evolving cyberthreat, but that a government role in cybersecurity is warranted in cases where high transaction costs or legal barriers lead to significant coordination problems. Thus the DHS contends that a public–private engagement is the foundation of *The National Strategy to Secure Cyberspace*. The public–private engagement will eventually take a variety of forms and will address awareness, training, technologic improvements, vulnerability remediation, and recovery operations.

Regardless of what the government may do or say, the bottom line in this situation is that the private sector owns and operates more than 95 percent of the cyberinfrastructure of the United States. This means that the private sector will be targets of a large number of malicious code attacks and will need to bear the cost of defending against attacks and restoring systems if defensive measures are not successful. This chapter provides a basic understanding of how and why the cyberinfrastructure is affected by malicious code attacks, including the following:

- Why malicious code attacks are dangerous
- The impact of malicious code attacks on corporate security
- Why malicious code attacks are so successful
- How flaws and vulnerabilities in software increase the costs of defending against malicious code attacks
- How weaknesses in system and network configurations software increase the costs of defending against malicious code attacks
- Why social engineering works so well for attackers
- How human error and foolishness aids attackers
- Why hackers, thieves, and spies target corporate networks

WHY MALICIOUS CODE ATTACKS ARE DANGEROUS

There are substantial economic consequences of computer crimes that involve malicious code attacks, unauthorized intrusion into networks and computer systems, and denial-of-service attacks. Dale L. Watson, Executive Assistant Director, Counter-terrorism and Counterintelligence of the FBI, testified before the Senate Select Committee on Intelligence on February 6, 2002. Watson pointed out that during the past several years, the FBI had identified a wide array of cyberthreats, ranging from defacement of Web sites by juveniles to sophisticated intrusions sponsored by foreign powers.

Watson pointed out that some of these incidents pose more significant threats than others. The theft of national security information from a government agency or the interruption of electrical power to a major metropolitan area obviously would have greater consequences for national security, public safety, and the economy than the defacement of a Web site. But even the less serious categories have real consequences and, ultimately, can undermine public confidence in Web-based commerce and violate privacy or property rights. An attack on a Web site that closes down an e-commerce site can have disastrous consequences for a Web-based business. An intrusion that results in the theft of millions of credit card numbers from an online vendor can result in significant financial loss and, more broadly, reduce consumers' willingness to engage in e-commerce.

Watson contended that beyond criminal threats, cyberspace also faces a variety of significant national security threats, including increasing threats from terrorists. Terrorist groups are increasingly using new information technology and the Internet to formulate plans, raise funds, spread propaganda, and engage in secure communications. Cyberterrorism—meaning the use of cybertools to shut down critical national infrastructures (e.g., energy, transportation, or government operations) for the purpose of coercing or intimidating a government or civilian population—is clearly an emerging threat.

In testimony on April 8, 2003, before the Subcommittee on Technology, Information Policy, Intergovernmental Relations and the Census of the United States House of Representatives, the General Accounting Office (GAO) reported on computer system attacks. The GAO testimony included several examples of attacks:

•   On February 11, 2003, the National Infrastructure Protection Center (NIPC) issued an advisory on an increase in global hacking activities as a result of the rising tensions between the United States and Iraq. This advisory noted that during a time of international tension, illegal cyberactivity often escalates. This includes spamming, Web page defacements, and denial-of-service attacks. The advisory pointed out that attacks may have one of several objectives, including political activism targeting Iraq or those sympathetic to Iraq by self-described patriot hackers. Other purposes may be politically oriented attacks targeting U.S. systems by those opposed to any potential conflict with

Iraq. The attacks could also be criminal activity masquerading or using the current crisis to further personal goals.

- The Cooperative Association for Internet Data Analysis (CAIDA) observed that on January 25, 2003, the Oracle SQL Slammer worm (also known as Sapphire) infected more than 90 percent of vulnerable computers worldwide within 10 minutes of its release on the Internet. At that time, Slammer held the honor of being the fastest computer worm in history. Slammer doubled in size every 8.5 seconds and achieved its full scanning rate (55 million scans per second) after about 3 minutes. It caused considerable harm through network outages and such unforeseen consequences as canceled airline flights and automated teller machine (ATM) failures. The success of Slammer was far from necessary because a software patch that would have prevented Slammer's spread had been available since July 2002.

- In November 2002, a British computer administrator was indicted on charges that included breaking into 92 computer networks that belonged to the Pentagon, private companies, and the National Aeronautics and Space Administration (NASA). The break-ins occurred over a period of one year and caused about $900,000 in damage. According to the Justice Department, these attacks were one of the largest hacks ever perpetrated against the U.S. military. The attacker used his home computer and automated software available on the Internet to scan tens of thousands of computers on military networks looking for ones that had known vulnerabilities.

- On October 21, 2002, the NIPC reported that all of the 13 root-name servers that provide the primary roadmap for almost all Internet communications were targeted in a massive distributed denial-of-service attack. Seven of the servers failed to respond to legitimate network traffic, and two others failed intermittently during the attack.

- In August 2001, attacks referred to as Code Red, Code Red II, and SirCam affected millions of computer users, shut down Web sites, slowed Internet service, and disrupted business and government operations.

- In September 2001, the Nimda worm appeared, which used a combination of some of the most successful attack methods of Code Red II and the 1999 Melissa virus, allowing it to spread widely in a short amount of time. Security experts estimate that Code Red, Sircam, and Nimda caused billions of dollars in damage.

Although these situations and attacks are dramatic in and of themselves, it is important to understand that malicious code attack methods are constantly evolving. Attackers look for new vulnerabilities and new ways to exploit existing vulnerabilities. Attackers also learn fast, and many of them share their learned lessons with other attackers. Also bear in mind that many new people and types of groups are getting involved in attacks—some for fun, others in pursuit of their political or social agendas, and others motivated by economic gain.

The result of this combination of circumstances is that organizations must not only defend against the attack methods and attackers of today, but they must also be on guard for new methods and new attackers. This, in turn, means that computer and network security will be an ongoing challenge and expense.

IMPACT OF MALICIOUS CODE ATTACKS ON CORPORATE SECURITY

When a malicious code attack occurs, the focus on restoring operations as quickly as possible usually overrides the desire to collect data on the direct costs to respond, the loss of productivity, or other types of impact that a malicious code attack has on an organization. But understanding the costs associated with malicious code attacks and the impact that attacks can have on their organizations is what enables managers to make decisions as to how much to invest in countermeasures.

Although the methodology required to track time expenditures and corresponding cost for an organization is straightforward, many organizations are unsure how to measure a decline in productivity that results from a malicious code attack. The impact of a malicious code attack on an organization can also be viewed in terms of when the impact may occur:

- *Immediate economic impact* can include damage to systems that requires human intervention to repair or replace, disruption of business operations, and delays in transactions and cash flow.

- *Short-term economic impact* can include loss of contracts with other organizations in supply chains or the loss of retail sales, negative impact on an organization's reputation, and hindrance to developing new business.

- *Long-term economic impact* can include a decline in market valuation and/or stock price, erosion of investor confidence, and reduced goodwill value.

Table 1.1 shows several ways to measure the impact of malicious code attacks on an organization. Several of the items shown in the table are relatively easy to calculate. The costs of direct damage to an organization's computer systems and the cost to repair damage or restore systems and functionality can be provided by IT staff or contractors who are responsible for responding to attacks.

Table 1.1   Impact of Malicious Code Attack on an Organization.

Direct damage to target organization's computer systems
Cost to repair damage or restore target organization's systems and functionality
Decrease in productivity of employees in target organization
Delays in order processing or customer service in target organization
Decrease in productivity in customer's organization because of delays in target organization
Delays in customer's business because of delays in target organization
Negative impact on local economies where target organization is located
Negative impact on local economies where target organization's customers are located
Negative impact on value for individual investors in target organization
Negative impact on value of investment funds holding target organization securities
Negative impact on regional economies where target organization, customer, or investor organizations are located
Negative impact on national economies where target organization, customer, or investor organizations are located

Source: *Implementing Homeland Security in Enterprise IT,* Michael Erbschloe (Digital Press, 2003)

Decreases in productivity of employees or delays in order processing or customer service responses can be tracked and calculated by department managers. Experience shows that department managers may balk at the request for such data because they are so focused on getting operations running smoothly again after an attack. One motivator that managers can use with those who may resist is that the data they provide will help determine how much should be spent on defensive measures in order to reduce the possibility of future attacks.

Managing the supply chain system in business and manufacturing organizations has become a standard practice. Collecting data on business delays or a decrease in productivity in a customer's organization because of delays caused by an attack on your systems may not be relevant for all organizations. But if it is a problem, your salespeople, order processors, or customer service representatives are likely to hear about it. If your organization has customers who could be affected by delays in your organization, it is prudent to determine if an attack has an impact. This could help determine how much should be spent on defenses.

Other measures of impact are more complex and more difficult to collect data on. A negative impact on local economies where an organization or its customers are located could certainly occur in the event of a severe attack. The other impacts listed in Table 1.1 may very well occur if major information warfare attacks are launched against a country or region. Corporate managers should focus their attention on the areas that affect operations and customer service in order to decrease the impact of larger-scale attacks in the future.

WHY MALICIOUS CODE ATTACKS WORK

Many people blame computer manufacturers and software producers for making and selling systems that can be attacked so easily. There is no doubt that hardware and software companies have some responsibility for making their products more securable, but not all of the blame can be cast on the computer industry. There are many reasons why malicious code attacks are successful, including the following:

- Flaws in software design
- Vulnerabilities caused by insecure system and network configurations
- Social engineering methods used by attackers

- Human error and unaware computer users
- Persistence on the part of hackers, thieves, and spies

Reducing vulnerabilities related to these causes is a significant challenge for any organization. Guidance on how to overcome many IT problems can be found in *Socially Responsible IT Management*. This book explains 10 principles of social responsibility and how they can help eliminate many of the IT-related problems that organizations now face. Several of the principles directly affect an organization's ability to deal with IT security problems. The 10 principles are shown in Table 1.2.

Staffing is one of the key challenges in managing IT resources and the security of those resources. If IT departments and functions are not appropriately staffed, an organization puts itself at risk in many areas, including greater vulnerability to security breaches, poorly functioning equipment, improper intellectual property management, and inadequately performing applications.

Turnover in IT departments is also a major impediment to smoothly managing security efforts. Establishing a fair compensation plan for IT employees

Table 1.2   Principles of Socially Responsible IT Management.

Number	Principle
1	Staff IT departments appropriately.
2	Compensate IT workers fairly.
3	Train computer users adequately.
4	Provide ergonomic user environments.
5	Maintain secure and virus-free computer systems.
6	Safeguard the privacy of information.
7	Manage intellectual property ethically.
8	Utilize energy-efficient technology.
9	Recycle used computer equipment properly.
10	Support efforts to reduce the digital divide.

Source: *Socially Responsible IT Management*, Michael Erbschloe (Digital Press, 2002)

can mitigate turnover and the loss of key personnel. A 20 percent reduction in turnover in an IT department can save hundreds of thousands of dollars in recruitment costs. Reduced turnover can also help keep projects on schedule because work will not be disrupted when staff leaves and replacements are recruited and brought up to speed on a project. Fairly compensated workers are also more motivated and will work more diligently to address security, privacy, and performance issues facing all organizations.

Training computer users is an important step in ensuring that an organization gets the best return on investment from its information technology. Training is also essential to a successful security program. Many positive results are achieved from adequately training users, including the following:

- Users feel more confident and will try new approaches to completing tasks.

- Users have a better understanding of what information technology can do for the organization.

- Help desk calls for simple problem solving decline, allowing support staff to spend time on more critical issues.

- Coworkers are not coerced into providing support to undertrained users and are able to focus more on their jobs.

- Accidental security breaches can be reduced.

- The incidents of viruses entering a corporate network can be reduced when users are trained on basic prevention skills.

Flaws in Software

There is considerable debate about software quality and the responsibility of software producers to develop and sell more secure software. There are also numerous perspectives on developer responsibility. Some developers believe that security is the responsibility of the organizations that deploy their products. Many users, however, believe that software products should be secure right out of the box. It is not likely that this debate will end any time soon.

One thing that is certain is that organizations cannot wait for the debate to be settled. More than 3,000 vulnerabilities have been discovered during the last three years. Every month, about 200 new software vulnerabilities are discovered. This means that organizations need to keep up to date about vulnerabilities in the products they use. Once vulnerabilities are announced, steps must be taken to install patches or seek alternative products for high-risk applications.

As was indicated earlier in this chapter, some malicious code attacks did not have to happen. In early 2003 when the Oracle SQL Slammer worm struck, a patch had been available for six months that would have prevented the worm from attacking a system. Many people cast blame for Slammer on system managers for not having patched their systems. There is some validity to that position, but keep in mind that Slammer or a similar worm could have been written to take advantage of vulnerabilities that the patch did not address. With 200 new vulnerabilities being discovered every month, there is always something for an attacker to take advantage of that can cause your organization pain and discomfort.

The main thing to keep in mind is that software flaws and vulnerabilities are chronic. They will never go away. This is one of the conditions that make computer security an ongoing and never-ending process. This point should be constantly reiterated to managers and computer users.

Weaknesses in System and Network Configurations

Another one of the major causes of vulnerable systems is how computers and networking devices are configured when they are installed. Several years ago, it was determined that the out-of-the-box settings for many operating systems introduced an unnecessary weakness into a computing environment. Although the out-of-the-box settings allowed the system to function adequately, the settings were not optimized for security.

Ongoing configuration is generally weak in most organizations. There is often a lack of documentation regarding how many computers and network devices are configured once they have been installed. Far too many organizations do a poor job of maintaining documentation about their technology. This is caused, in part, by a lack of discipline in IT departments. Another cause of poor documentation is a common trend of understaffing IT departments. Far too many of the problems caused by weak configurations and slowness in patching software products to reduce vulnerabilities can be tied back to inadequate IT staffing.

Information on security-focused configurations is not difficult to find, and there are several sources of information. Manufacturers can provide advice through their help desks or system documentation. Security organizations like

SANS (see www.sans.org) also provide advice as well as training to address configuration issues.

Social Engineering

One of the greatest vulnerabilities to malicious code attacks that any organization has is the employees who use computers. People can be easily duped into unwittingly and unknowingly helping an attack succeed, and attackers who use malicious code as a weapon know this to be true. Social engineering techniques range from simple and straightforward tricks to incredibly complex methods of deception that require several steps.

In early May 2000, a simple social engineering trick was used to get people to open an e-mail that launched a malicious code attack that resulted in e-mail systems around the world being clogged with messages for as long as a week. An e-mail with the subject line "I love you" was enough to get thousands of people to open the message and unknowingly launch an attack from their computers. Once the e-mail was opened, it could mail itself to the e-mail addresses in the address book of the host computer. This was a major and virtually global malicious code attack. Some e-mail systems were closed down for days. One U.S. government agency was barraged with more than 7 million "I love you" e-mail messages. Figure 1.1 shows how an e-mail virus spreads.

In early 2001, another famous socially engineered malicious code attack was perpetrated using an e-mail that offered the recipient free nude photos of tennis star Anna Kournikova. Other deceptive e-mails that use the recipient's

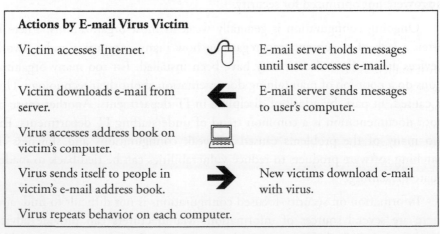

Actions by E-mail Virus Victim

Victim accesses Internet.

E-mail server holds messages until user accesses e-mail.

Victim downloads e-mail from server.

E-mail server sends messages to user's computer.

Virus accesses address book on victim's computer.

Virus sends itself to people in victim's e-mail address book.

New victims download e-mail with virus.

Virus repeats behavior on each computer.

Figure 1.1. *How E-mail Viruses Spread*

computer to launch an attack have had subject lines that said they were virus alerts, information on security flaws, locations of free pornography, or information about an e-commerce Web site order. Social engineering techniques are always evolving, and attackers utilize techniques that take advantage of popular cultural, musical, artistic, or marketing trends.

Human Error and Foolishness

In addition to falling victim to social engineering tricks of attackers, computer users can do a wide variety of things to unknowingly or unwittingly enable a malicious code attack. Common mistakes include opening e-mail attachments from unknown senders, visiting Web sites that are infected with worms, and loading documents from floppy disks that result in malicious code being transferred to desktop computers.

Most people do not understand their computers well enough to tell when an anomaly is occurring. When things start going wrong with their computers, most users do not know how to react. In most cases, computer problems are just technical in nature. However, when a worm or virus has damaged a system, errors or events that appear to be unknown technical problems can occur.

Employees can take several steps to help avert an attack. However, employees cannot be held responsible for these types of mistakes unless adequate training and documented policies and procedures have been provided for handling events that enable an attack. A model training program for users that is designed to help organizations reduce human errors that may enable an attack is provided in Chapter 8.

Hackers, Thieves, and Spies

Most malicious code attacks are not targeted at a specific organization. All of the cases that the GAO reported to Congress and the examples used to illustrate social engineering techniques were results of malicious code finding its way around the Internet unassisted. However, adversaries are capable of targeting a specific organization to damage systems, disrupt operations, or steal information. Trojans, backdoors, and spyware can be placed on systems by adversaries to assist them in accomplishing a specific mission. Figure 1.2 shows the sequence of events that occur when spyware is downloaded to a victim's computer.

In October 2001, the NIPC released a report entitled *Cyber Protests: The Threat to the U.S. Information Infrastructure*. The report stated that during the

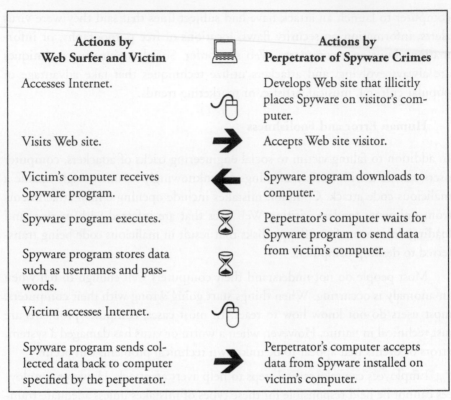

Actions by Web Surfer and Victim		Actions by Perpetrator of Spyware Crimes
Accesses Internet.		Develops Web site that illicitly places Spyware on visitor's computer.
Visits Web site.	→	Accepts Web site visitor.
Victim's computer receives Spyware program.	←	Spyware program downloads to computer.
Spyware program executes.	⌛	Perpetrator's computer waits for Spyware program to send data from victim's computer.
Spyware program stores data such as usernames and passwords.	⌛	
Victim accesses Internet.		
Spyware program sends collected data back to computer specified by the perpetrator.	→	Perpetrator's computer accepts data from Spyware installed on victim's computer.

Figure 1.2. *How Spyware Works*

last decade, protests and political activism on the Internet has generated a wide range of activity, including Web site defacements and denial-of-service attacks. Cyberprotesters have a wide range of goals or objectives. Some hackers want to expose government corruption or fundamental violation of human rights; others just want to hack and cause mischief for fun or to make a point. These politically motivated, computer-based attacks are usually described as *hacktivism*, a marriage of hacking and political activism. The report provided insight into numerous attacks that were directed at specific countries or organizations.

One high-profile incident occurred in May 1999 after the United States accidentally bombed the Chinese embassy in Belgrade, Yugoslavia, during the NATO air campaign. Several Web sites in the United States were defaced in the name of China, and massive e-mail campaigns were executed to gain sympathy and support for the Chinese cause. Government Web sites were primarily targeted. The Departments of Energy and the Interior and the National Park Service all suffered Web page defacements. In addition, the White House Web site was taken down for three days after it was continually mail bombed.

In April and May 2001, pro-Chinese hacktivists and cyberprotesters began a cyberassault on Web sites in the United States, which was prompted by an incident in which a Chinese fighter jet was lost at sea after colliding with a U.S. Navy reconnaissance aircraft. It also coincided with the two-year anniversary of the Chinese embassy bombing by the United States in Belgrade and the traditionally celebrated May Day and Youth Day in China. Led by the Honkers Union of China (HUC), pro-Chinese hackers defaced or crashed more than 100 seemingly random Web sites, mainly .gov and .com sites.

Organizations that already have well-organized adversary groups are probably at the highest risk for hacktivist attacks, but hackers and thieves do not have to belong to well-organized groups. They can be former employees or individuals who feel that they have been wronged in some way by the policies or behavior of individuals in an organization.

ACTION STEPS TO COMBAT MALICIOUS CODE ATTACKS

The material in this chapter shows that malicious code attacks have been and will continue to be a problem that organizations need to address. As steps are taken to defend against malicious code attacks, managers, planners, and technical staff should understand the following rudiments:

- Malicious code attacks have caused considerable damage and disruption and will grow in intensity in the future.

- The vulnerabilities in technology and flaws in software continue to grow rapidly, which requires ongoing diligence by IT staff responsible for countermeasures.

- The number and types of individuals who can use and may be motivated to use malicious code attacks as forms of protest or to commit crimes is growing.

- In addition to vulnerabilities in computer and networking technology, social engineering, human error, and a lack of knowledge on the part of computer users all help enable malicious code attacks.

Organizations can take several steps to help reduce the impact of malicious code attacks. Recommended steps are included at the end of each chapter. The following action items are helpful in implementing new malicious code attack countermeasures or evaluating existing countermeasures. The action steps listed in Table 1.3 are designed to help an organization determine what steps have been taken to prevent malicious code attacks.

One way to manage new or renewed efforts to develop measures to counter malicious code attacks is to establish a working group to evaluate how the organization is addressing the threat. The working group will be responsible for working with function departments, such as human resources and the IT department, to develop a comprehensive approach.

Table 1.3   Action Steps to Combat Malicious Code Attacks

Number	Action Step
1.1	Establish a working group to evaluate how the organization is addressing the threat of malicious code attacks.
1.2	Select members of the working group from IT, human resources, legal, and other departments.
1.3	Designate two co-chairs for the working group.
1.4	Convene the working group members to discuss how they can best organizes themselves to address the threat of malicious code attacks.
1.5	Have the working group set a timeline for activities based on the action steps contained in subsequent chapters of this book.

2

Types of Malicious Code

Malicious code comes in a wide variety of forms and is distributed through an ever-growing number of delivery mechanisms. In general, malicious code is any software that impedes the normal operation of a computer or networking device. This software most often executes without the user's consent.

It is widely recognized that attempting to eliminate all risks is nearly impossible, and any effort to do so will not likely be cost effective, let alone successful. A more achievable goal is to ensure that business risks are limited to an acceptable level. Risk management is an ongoing process of assessing risks to business as a first step in determining what type of security will be adequate. This principle is what guides the process of selecting countermeasures to malicious code attacks.

Understanding how malicious code works can help you develop defensive strategies, select computer security products, and train employees on how to identify potential threats. This chapter explains the various types of malicious code that have caused computer users problems in the past. As with other chapters, action steps are included at the end of the chapter to help your organization deploy countermeasures to reduce the impact of malicious code attacks. The explanations in this chapter are written at a basic, nontechnical level so they can be used in the training sessions recommended in Chapter 8. Types of malicious code covered in this chapter include the following:

- E-mail and other types of viruses

- Trojans and other backdoors

- Worms

- Blended threats

- Time bombs

- Spyware

- Adware

- Stealware

When a piece of malicious code starts infecting a large number of computers, it is said to be "in the wild." In contrast, a malicious code that has only been identified by antivirus researchers is said to be a "zoo virus," which resides predominantly in the malicious code collections of researchers. There are tens of thousands of known viruses, worms, and Trojans, but remarkably very few actually cause any concern. The *wild list*, or *threat list*, refers to malicious code that is wandering around the Internet infecting computers. An archive of wild lists and information about the organization that compiles and maintains the lists are available at www.wildlist.org.

The threat level or pervasiveness of malicious code refers to its potential to spread and infect computers. The typical classifications are no, low, medium, and high threat. The no-threat rating is given to malicious code that may not function well or is a hoax. The low-threat rating is usually given to malicious code that requires human assistance in replicating and moving from computer to computer. The medium-threat rating is usually given to malicious code that has slow infection speed and does little, if any, damage. The high-threat rating is given to malicious code that can replicate at great speed or can do considerable damage.

E-MAIL VIRUSES AND MISCELLANEOUS VIRUSES

A virus is a computer program that initiates an action on a computer without the user's consent. There have been tens of thousands of viruses circulating around the Internet, and hundreds more are created and released every year. In addition, writers often modify existing viruses to perform tasks different than the original author assigned to the virus. This can also involve improving the original virus's functionality and ability.

In general, computer viruses replicate and spread from one system to another. Many viruses merely replicate and clog e-mail systems. Some computer viruses have what is called a *malicious payload*, which is code that can execute commands on computers such as deleting or corrupting files or disabling computer security software. In addition, some computer viruses can attach themselves to another block of code to facilitate propagation. Viruses generally have the following components:

- A *replication mechanism* that allows reproduction and enables the virus to move from one computer to other computers

- A *trigger* that is designed to execute the replication mechanism or the task of the virus

- A *task* or *group of tasks* that execute on a computer to destroy or alter files, change computer settings or configurations, or otherwise hinder or impede the operations of a computer or networking device

These three components can take on a wide variety of forms and behaviors. Replication mechanisms can vary considerably, and the virus can be designed to execute an endless combination and variety of tasks. Some popular types of viruses include the following:

- A *boot sector virus* infects the first sector of a floppy disk or hard drive. The first sector contains the master boot record that enables the configuration of a computer when electric power is turned on and the operating system launches. Thus, when the computer is turned on, the virus launches immediately and is loaded into memory, enabling it to control the computer. In general, a boot sector virus infects any disk that is placed in the floppy drive. A boot sector does not move over network connections to other computers.

- *File-deleting viruses* have the tasks of deleting specifically named files such as those that execute basic instructions or enable computers to launch applications. Other file-deleting viruses are designed to delete certain types of files such as word processing documents, spreadsheets, or graphic files.

- *File-infecting viruses* often attach themselves to executable files with the extension .com, .exe, .dll, .ovr, or .ovl. Thus, when the file is run, the virus spreads by attaching itself to the executable files. These viruses are similar to appender viruses that insert a copy of their code at the end of a file. *Content-embedded viruses* are file-infecting viruses that reside in or are attached to graphic files, html pages, video files, or sound files.

- *Macro viruses* can spread through macro instructions found in office applications such as Microsoft Word or Excel spreadsheets. These macros are usually stored as part of the document or spreadsheet and can travel to other systems if those files are attached to an e-mail message, placed on a floppy disk, or copied onto a file server for other people to access.

- *Mass mailers* work within the e-mail programs on a computer and generally replicate by e-mailing themselves to the addresses stored in the address book of the e-mail program. There is a difference in threat level between mass mailers and slow mailers. Both may use the same method of replication, but a mass mailer is usually considered more of a threat because of its replication speed and the extent that it can clog up e-mail servers and overwhelm computer users by drowning their e-mail boxes with excessive messages. In addition, a medium- or high-level threat mass mailer will also attempt to drown those people for which there is an e-mail address in an infected individual's e-mail address book. Figure 2.1 shows how a mass mailer replicates.

- *Multiple-characteristic viruses* can have a combination of the virus types described here as well as an ever-growing combination of traits, capabilities, and tasks.

- *Polymorphic viruses* can change their appearance every time they infect a different system. They often successfully hide from the virus protection software.

- *Stealth viruses* hide from operating system or virus protection software. These viruses can make changes to file sizes or directory structure. Stealth viruses are similar in nature to antiheuristic viruses that malicious code writers design to elude the heuristic detection capabilities of virus protection software. Heuristics for malicious code detectors are rule based, which means that even if the malicious code has not been seen before, it is not possible to detect every variant of existing viruses.

- *Socially engineered e-mail message subject lines* can be used to prompt computer users to open and thus execute a virus that can have any of the characteristics described here as well as an ever-growing combination of traits, capabilities, and tasks.

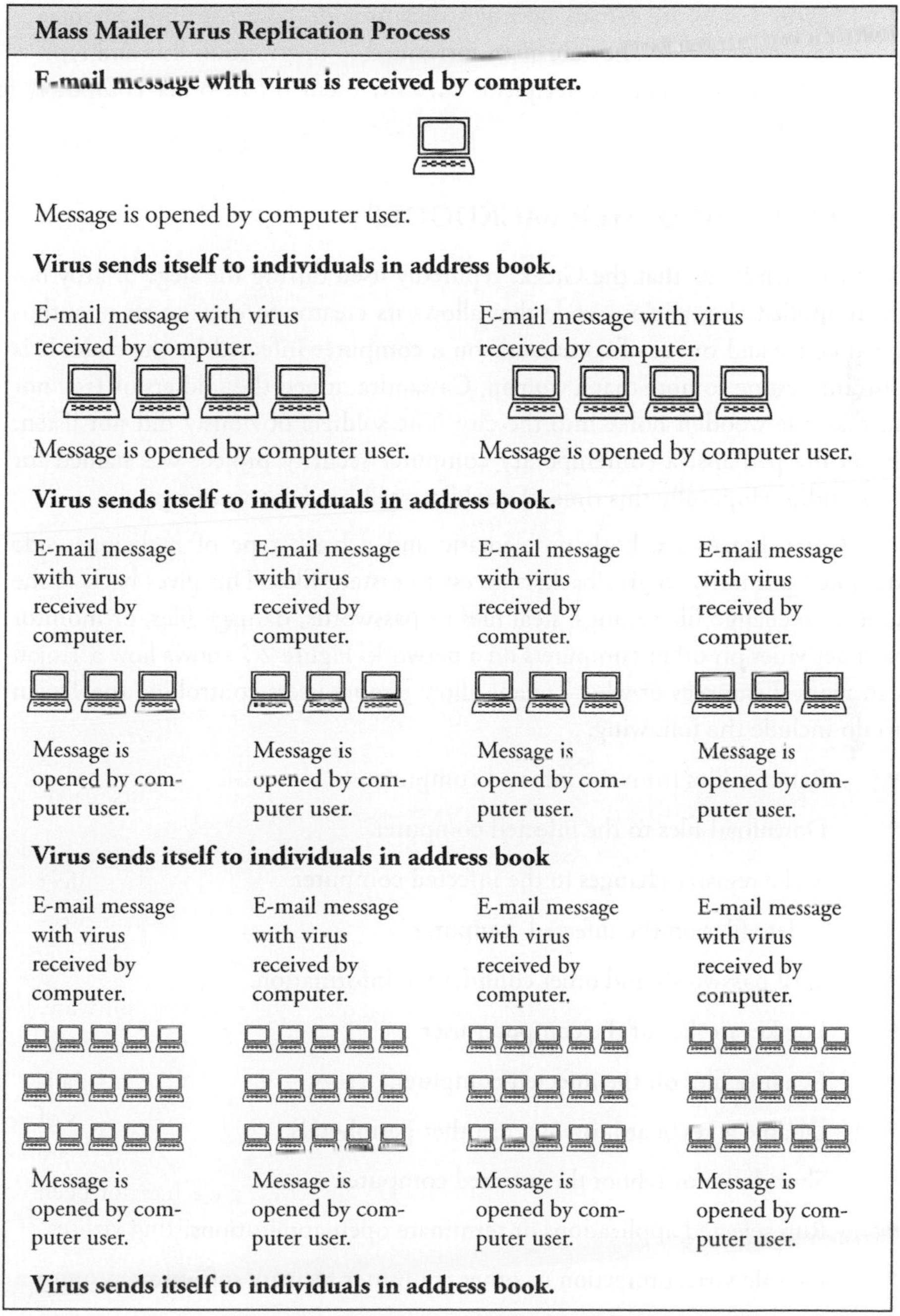

Mass Mailer Virus Replication Process

E-mail message with virus is received by computer.

Message is opened by computer user.

Virus sends itself to individuals in address book.

E-mail message with virus received by computer.

E-mail message with virus received by computer.

Message is opened by computer user.

Message is opened by computer user.

Virus sends itself to individuals in address book.

E-mail message with virus received by computer.

E-mail message with virus received by computer.

E-mail message with virus received by computer.

E-mail message with virus received by computer.

Message is opened by computer user.

Message is opened by computer user.

Message is opened by computer user.

Message is opened by computer user.

Virus sends itself to individuals in address book

E-mail message with virus received by computer.

E-mail message with virus received by computer.

E-mail message with virus received by computer.

E-mail message with virus received by computer.

Message is opened by computer user.

Message is opened by computer user.

Message is opened by computer user.

Message is opened by computer user.

Virus sends itself to individuals in address book.

Figure 2.1. *How Mass Mailers Work*

- *Virus hoaxes* are e-mail messages that provide false warnings about a computer virus. They are often forwarded to distribution lists and typically request that the recipients forward them on to other computer users as a service.

TROJANS AND OTHER BACKDOORS

The wooden horse that the Greeks reputedly used during the siege of Troy has been applied to malicious code that allows its creator to execute an unauthorized command or set of commands on a computer infected by the code. It is also interesting to note that a woman, Cassandra, urged the soldiers of Troy not to take the wooden horse into the city. The soldiers obviously did not listen. Ironically perhaps, a contemporary computer security project was named for Cassandra. Hopefully this time, the soldiers will heed the warning.

Trojan horses are both problematic and a basic type of malicious code designed primarily to give hackers access to system files. This gives hackers the ability to change file settings, steal files or passwords, damage files, or monitor user activities on other computers on a network. Figure 2.2 shows how a Trojan can work. Examples of what Trojans allow remote users controlling the Trojan to do include the following:

- Remove files from the infected computer.
- Download files to the infected computer.
- Make registry changes to the infected computer.
- Delete files on the infected computer.
- Steal passwords and other confidential information.
- Log keystrokes of the computer user.
- Rename files on the infected computer.
- Disable a keyboard, mouse, or other peripherals.
- Shut down or reboot the infected computer.
- Run selected applications or terminate open applications.
- Disable virus protection or other computer security software.

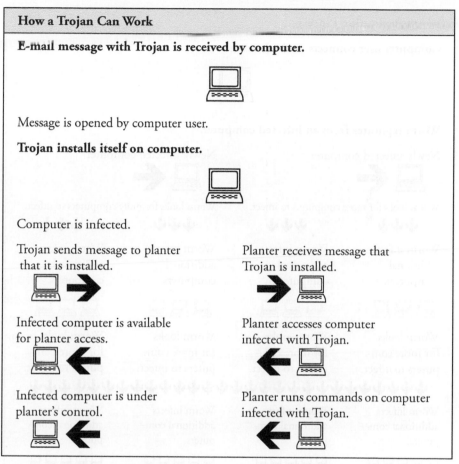

How a Trojan Can Work

E-mail message with Trojan is received by computer.

Message is opened by computer user.

Trojan installs itself on computer.

Computer is infected.

Trojan sends message to planter that it is installed.

Planter receives message that Trojan is installed.

Infected computer is available for planter access.

Planter accesses computer infected with Trojan.

Infected computer is under planter's control.

Planter runs commands on computer infected with Trojan.

Figure 2.2. *How a Trojan Can Work*

WORMS

A worm is a malicious program that originates on a single computer and searches for other computers connected through a local area network (LAN) or Internet connection. When a worm finds another computer, it replicates itself onto that computer and continues to look for other connected computers on which to replicate. A worm continues to attempt to replicate itself indefinitely or until a self-timing mechanism halts the process. Figure 2.3 illustrates one of the ways a worm can work.

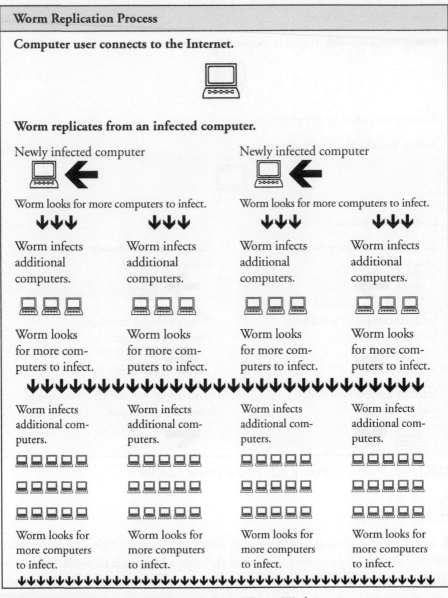

Figure 2.3. *How Worms Work*

BLENDED THREATS

Malicious code that is referred to as a blended threat is code that can replicate itself in more than one manner, can have more than one type of trigger, and can have multiple task capabilities. A blended threat is often able to move around

---

How a Time Bomb Can Work

Programmer places time bomb code on computer.

Computer continues to function normally for several days or weeks.

Date and time trigger is reached.

Computer malfunctions or fails.

Figure 2.4. *How a Time Bomb Can Work*

the Internet using e-mail virus capabilities as well as worm capabilities. A blended threat attack can also plant a Trojan on a computer. The trigger can be set off by an e-mail program action or a Web surfing action. Malicious code writers have become sophisticated in blending the characteristics and capabilities of multiple threat types. This is part of the ongoing knowledge-building process in the malicious code–writing community.

TIME BOMBS

One of the first forms of malicious code was a time bomb (or logic bomb), which, when installed, is a dormant code that can be triggered at a future date by a specific event or circumstance. Triggers can be a specific date and time or even a cumulative number of system starts. Many disgruntled programmers have planted time bombs to retaliate against employers. Time bombs have also been installed in extortion attempts. Figure 2.4 illustrates one of the ways a time bomb can work.

SPYWARE

The term *spyware* is used to describe any computer technology that gathers information about a person or organization without their knowledge or con-

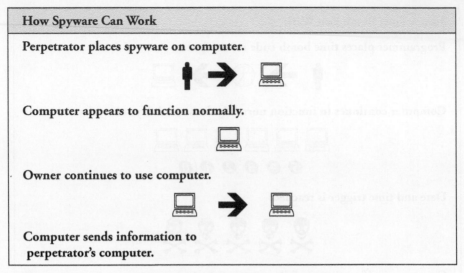

Figure 2.5. *How Spyware Can Work*

sent. Spyware can be installed on a computer through several covert means, including as part of a software virus or as the result of adding a new program. Note that the terms spyware, stealware, and adware are sometimes used to describe the same or similar types of malicious code. Several states, including Utah, Iowa, California, and New York, are working on legislation to ban or control spyware. In addition, the U.S. Congress is also considering new laws.

Spyware is used to gather information such as recorded keystrokes (passwords), a list of Web sites visited by the user, or applications and operating systems that are installed on the computer. Spyware can also collect names, credit card numbers, and other personal information. It is usually placed on a computer to gather information about a user that is later sold to advertisers and other interested parties. The information gathered by spyware is often combined with other databases to create profiles of individuals, families, work groups, or even entire companies. Such profiles are mainly used for direct marketing purposes. Figure 2.5 illustrates how spyware typically works.

ADWARE

Several advertising networks have been accused of using a form of malicious code called *Web bugs* to collect information about computer users to assist in the compilation of personal profiles. These bugs can collect information about the Web sites that Internet users visit and what they do at those Web sites. The

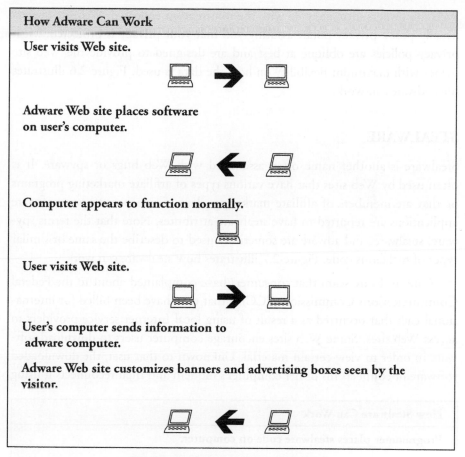

How Adware Can Work

User visits Web site.

**Adware Web site places software
on user's computer.**

Computer appears to function normally.

User visits Web site.

**User's computer sends information to
adware computer.**

**Adware Web site customizes banners and advertising boxes seen by the
visitor.**

Figure 2.6. *How Adware Can Work*

information can be stored in databases and used to select what types of banners or advertisements users are shown.

Large Web sites that request or require information from visitors in exchange for custom pages or specialized sales approaches usually require that visitors accept cookies onto their computers. The type of cookie that the Web site sends to the visitor's computer is sometimes referred to as a *Web bug*. Note that the terms spyware, stealware, and adware are sometimes used to describe the same or similar types of malicious code.

The Web sites that are using adware code claim that they take these actions to improve the customer experience. The flip side of that perspective is that if users have a better experience, they will spend more money at the Web site. This tactic seems harmless enough on the surface, but the danger is in what the

Web site owners ultimately do with the information collected. Web site owners usually post a privacy policy assuring you that your privacy is protected. Most privacy policies are oblique at best and are designed to provide the Web site owner with maximum flexibility on how the data is used. Figure 2.6 illustrates how adware can work.

STEALWARE

Stealware is another name often associated with Web bugs or spyware. It is often used by Web sites that have various types of affiliate marketing programs or that are members of affiliate marketing plans. Some peer-to-peer software applications are reported to have stealware attributes. Note that the terms spyware, stealware, and adware are sometimes used to describe the same or similar types of malicious code. Figure 2.7 illustrates how stealware can work.

One stealware scam that consumers have complained about to the Federal Communications Commission (FCC) is that they have been billed for international calls that occurred as a result of using local Internet service providers to access Web sites. Some Web sites encourage computer users to download software in order to view certain material. Unknown to that user, the downloaded software disconnects his or her computer's modem and then reconnects it using

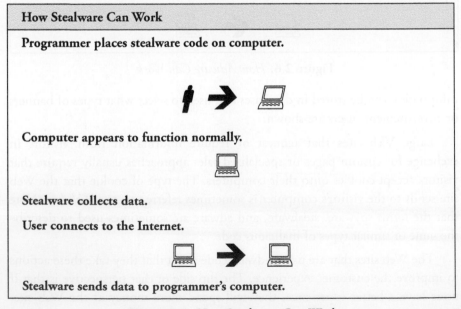

Figure 2.7. *How Stealware Can Work*

an international long-distance number. The result is that the modem may actually be placing a call to as far away as Chad, Madagascar, or other countries, and the computer user may be billed for an international call.

Some Web sites may be advertised as free and uncensored or may allow information to be downloaded. However, a pop-up window with a disclaimer should appear. The disclaimer usually reveals information on possible charges or rerouting of the Web site. It may say: "You will be disconnected from your local Internet access number and reconnected to an international location." It is important that computer users read the disclaimer to learn what charges will be assessed before they click the box. If they still choose to download, users should be prepared to receive a phone bill with high international toll charges. There may also be charges from a nontelecommunications company that provides a billing service to the Web site in question.

ACTION STEPS TO COMBAT MALICIOUS CODE ATTACKS

The material in this chapter shows the types of malicious code that have been created over the last several years. As steps are taken to defend against malicious code attacks, managers, planners, trainers, and technical staff should understand the types of malicious code that exist and the impact they can have on an organization, including these basic concepts:

- There are a wide variety of malicious code types. In order to defend against attacks, organizations need to deploy multiple defensive methods to protect computers and networking devices.

- Malicious code writers are constantly evolving to take advantage of new exploits and current social engineering techniques. In order to keep up to date with the latest trends, organizations must constantly update security processes and training material.

- Many malicious code attacks can be inadvertently launched when computer users fall into traps set by attackers. Users must be trained to recognize potential hazards.

Organizations can take several steps to help reduce the impact of malicious code attacks. Recommended steps are included at the end of each chapter. The following action items are helpful in implementing new malicious code attack countermeasures or evaluating existing countermeasures. The actions steps listed in Table 2.1 are designed to help an organization build knowledge on how to counter malicious code attacks.

Table 2.1   Action Steps to Combat Malicious Code Attacks.

Number	Action Step
2.1	Assign working group members responsibility for the tasks outlined in the action steps for this chapter.
2.2	Determine who in the organization has any responsibility for preventing malicious code attacks.
2.3	Determine how the organization makes decisions about how much to spend to prevent malicious code attacks.
2.4	Collect information on the number of attacks and the nature of the attacks that have occurred over the last two years.
2.5	Collect information on how much damage or disruption malicious code attacks have caused in the organization.
2.6	Determine if an attack on the organization has caused problems in delivering goods or services to customers or clients.
2.7	Determine if computer users have had any training about preventing or reporting malicious code attack.
2.8	Compile the results of the inquiries and data collection into a brief report for use by the malicious code attack working group.
2.9	Convene the working group to discuss the results of the information-collection activities in the action steps for this chapter.

3
Review of Malicious Code Incidents

The history of malicious code has technical, political, economic, and social aspects. On the technical side, the one lesson that has been repeated over and over again is that as technology advances and evolves, so do malicious code writers. No technology will ever be safe from malicious code writers because they cannot resist the challenge, and the basic axiom is that geeks never give up.

The political side of this history is rooted mostly in the near-absolute failure of governments and law enforcement agencies to counter malicious code attacks and apprehend and prosecute malicious code writers. It is extremely difficult to trace the origin of a malicious code attack. This provides us with another axiom: Geeks can be extremely elusive.

The economics of malicious code attacks are absolutely staggering even by the most conservative estimates. Billions and billions of dollars year after year are consumed to protect against malicious code attacks and clean up the mess when the defenses fail, as they most often do. But as with all things, capitalism has created an entire industrial complex built on the foundations of the previous two axioms. Virus protection and computer security software companies have thrived. Thousands of people are employed around the world to fight off the malicious code attacks that are created by perhaps only a few hundred people. Axiom number three: The actions of the few can result in jobs for many.

The social side of malicious code attacks is perhaps the most fascinating. Do you remember when you were in high school and college? There was the geek: Shunned by the football team and cheerleaders, ignored by the pretty girls, never invited to parties, and could not have gotten a date even if he had been invited. Now many of you are grown, but you still have geeks in your life: It could be the guy at work who takes care of the computers or the kid next door or around the corner. Most geeks are treated pretty poorly by many people who see themselves as being socially superior. Guess what? They got you back. They will get you back next year and the year after that and the year after that. Your computer will forever be under attack. The final and most significant axiom of this chapter: Geeks could rule the world!

This chapter provides a brief, nontechnical history of some of the most dramatic malicious code attacks to date. This material is written at a basic level to make it usable in the model training process provided in Chapter 8. The examples of attacks help illustrate the potential severity of an attack and what can happen to your organization if adequate countermeasures are not deployed. For the purposes of training, it would be helpful to communicate the experience of your organization and how you responded to these global events.

HISTORIC TIDBITS

Imagine a malicious code attack that could flood the Internet with 55 million blasts of data per second and in 10 minutes colonize almost all of the computers that are vulnerable to its exploits. Think about an attack that could slow down the response time of a 911 system or cripple air traffic control for major airports. It has all happened, and it is likely to happen again. In China during 2003, about 85 percent of all computers were infected with a computer virus during the year. Now can you imagine why such attacks occur?

Malicious code writers are hostile toward Microsoft, the most successful software company in the world, with more than 90 percent of desktop computers running Microsoft products. Malicious code writers have beaten on and embarrassed Microsoft into humiliation in the eyes of geeks around the world. Malicious code writers have forced Microsoft to spend billions of dollars trying to make its products more secure. This money could have been used by Microsoft to pursue its goal of world market domination and pay even larger bonuses to executives and larger dividends to stockholders. Microsoft is not happy and has established a $5 million fund to pay for information leading to the capture of writers who target Windows machines. One such effort was a bounty of $250,000 for the creators of Blaster, Sobig.F, and MyDoom.B, which struck in 2003 and 2004.

Many people think that malicious code virus writers should be rounded up, arrested, prosecuted, and jailed. However, most countries do not have laws that make writing malicious code illegal. Some of the more interesting dates in the history of malicious code are shown in Table 3-1.

Attacks are constant, and they are increasing in number and severity. Attackers use various types of malicious code during the attack process. The United States Department of Defense (DoD) computer systems were attacked every day during the 1990s according to reports of the Defense Information Systems Agency (DISA). In 1995, there were as many as 250,000 attacks.

Table 3.1   Chronology of Malicious Code Events.

Year	Events
1949	Theories for self-replicating programs are first developed.
1981	Apple Viruses 1, 2, and 3 are some of the first viruses that spread through pirated computer games.
1983	Fred Cohen, while working on his dissertation, formally defines a computer virus as a computer program that can affect other computer programs by modifying them in such a way as to include a (possibly evolved) copy of itself.
1986	Pakistani Brain, the first boot sector virus, appears.
1987	The Lehigh virus appears as one of the first viruses that infect command.com files.
1988	Jerusalem is released into the wild to be activated every Friday the 13th, affecting.exe and .com files and deleting programs that run that day.
1988	Cornell graduate student Robert Morris Jr. releases the now-called Morris Worm, which exploited a flaw in the UNIX operating system and spread within days to more than 6,000 computers (about 15 percent of the Internet at that time).
1989	A teenager in Sophia, Bulgaria, releases the Dark Avenger virus, which destroyed data and contained references to lyrics from metal rock band Iron Maiden.
1991	Tequila, an early polymorphic virus, is launched.
1992	The Dark Avenger Mutation Engine (DAME) is made available, which can turn almost any virus into a polymorphic virus.

Table 3.1   Chronology of Malicious Code Events. (continued)

Year	Events
1994	One of the first virus hoaxes appears warning of a malicious virus that will erase an entire hard drive just by opening an e-mail with the subject line Good Times.
1995	The Word Concept virus spreads through Microsoft Word documents.
1998	The Chernobyl virus spreads through .exe files.
1999	Explore.zip attacks Microsoft products.
1999	The Melissa virus executes a macro in a document attached to an e-mail, which forwards the document to 50 people in the user's Outlook address book.
2000	The Love Bug, also known as the I Love You virus, sends itself out via Outlook and comes as a VBS attachment that overwrites files, including mp3, mp2, and .jpg files.
2001	The Anna Kournikova virus is released, which tricked e-mail users into clicking on an attachment that purported to be a nude photo of Russian tennis star Kournikova.
2001	SirCam uses e-mail to spread across the Internet rapidly.
2001	Code Red(s) worm their way onto hundreds of thousands of computers.
2001	Shortly after the September 11th attacks, the Nimda virus infects hundreds of thousands of computers in the world. The virus is one of the most sophisticated to date, with as many as five different methods of replicating and infecting systems.
2001	BadTrans, which is designed to capture passwords and credit card information, hits the Internet.
2002	There are more than 30,000 Web sites that provide virus programs and tools for launching attacks.
2003	Slammer becomes the fastest spreading worm to date, infecting 75,000 computers in approximately 10 minutes and doubling in size every 8.5 seconds.
2003	Blaster and Sobig break speed records for infection rates.

Table 3.1   Chronology of Malicious Code Events. (continued)

Year	Events
2004	MyDoom and other viruses plague the Internet at unprecedented speeds.

When DISA conducted vulnerability tests on DoD systems, it was found that 65 percent of the penetration tests were successful. Wright-Patterson Air Force Base told the United States General Accounting Office (GAO) that in 1995 it received 3,000 to 4,000 attempts to access information each month from countries all around the world. Many of these attacks were serious, and hackers not only stole or destroyed sensitive data and software, but they also installed backdoors into computer systems, which allows them to easily regain entry.

Rome Laboratory, an Air Force command and control research facility, reported that in March and April 1994, a British hacker known as Datastream Cowboy and another hacker called Kuji attacked the laboratory's computer systems more than 150 times. The two hackers used fairly common hacker techniques, including loading Trojans and sniffer programs, to break into the systems. At one point, the hackers took control of the lab's network, ultimately taking all 33 subnetworks offline for several days. Datastream Cowboy was caught in Great Britain by Scotland Yard, but Kuji was never caught and thus no one knows for sure what happened to the data stolen from Rome Lab.

THE MORRIS WORM

In 1988, a Cornell University graduate student named Robert Morris released an Internet worm program that spread through computers. It nearly halted the entire network because the computers that it did not affect immediately were not turned on or disconnected because of a fear of infection. At many national laboratories, workers were greeted at the gate by security guards handing out flyers informing them of the worm and warning them not to turn on their computers because of the fear of infection.

Robert Morris was the son of a computer security expert at the National Security Agency. He was charged with infecting 6,000 computers and was convicted of violating the computer Fraud and Abuse Act and was sentenced to three years' probation, 400 hours of community service, and a $10,000 fine. The computer trade press headlines read like a Hollywood tabloid. Information technology managers were aghast and called for harsher punishments.

It is likely that the worm infected more than 6,000 computers, and it certainly caused days of disruption. Estimates for the cleaning and lost productivity varied, but most were more than $100,000. This was the first big prosecution for a malicious code attack. The FBI, the prosecutors, and the courts were at that time inexperienced in how to deal with such cases. Many years later, it was rumored that Robert Morris went on to a major East Coast university to work on a doctoral degree.

One of the most significant impacts of the Morris Worm was that the Computer Emergency Response Team (CERT) was established by the Defense Advanced Research Projects Agency at Carnegie Mellon University's Software Engineering Institute, in Pittsburgh. The mission of CERT is to serve as a focal point to help resolve computer security incidents and vulnerabilities, to help others establish incident response capabilities, and to raise awareness of computer security issues and help people understand the steps they need to take to better protect their systems.

Bear in mind that the cold war was not yet over. The Morris Worm terrified a lot of people, especially because it seemed so easy for the worm to penetrate an essential defense and research network. CERT was activated in less than two weeks and now works closely with the DoD and the Department of Homeland Security (DHS).

MELISSA

In 1999, David Smith of New Jersey wrote the Melissa virus that replicated through e-mail and infected Microsoft Word documents. Melissa would replicate by sending itself to the first 50 addressees in the e-mail program of the recipient's computer. In a three-day period, Melissa infected more than 100,000 computers. Some organizations reported receiving tens of thousands of Melissa e-mail messages in less than an hour.

Melissa did have some limitations. Replication was very successful on computers that used Outlook 98 and Outlook 2000 for Windows e-mail programs. Melissa could use Microsoft Word 97 and Word 2000 for Windows and Word 98 for Macintosh to replicate by infecting documents. However, because earlier versions of Word, including Word 95, did not have such sophisticated macros, they could not be used to infect other documents. Outlook Express, or Outlook Lite as some called it, could not support Melissa's replication process.

Smith had two aliases: Vicodin for his virus writing and Doug Winter-spoon, which he used when he was posing as a legitimate virus expert. Smith had used the different aliases when posting to message boards, thus leaving a trail that helped investigators. In addition, Smith included his girlfriend's name in the code of Melissa. Smith was arrested in 1999 and eventually pleaded guilty to causing more than $80 million worth of damage when he released his Melissa virus on the Internet.

LOVE BUG

May 4, 2000 was one of the most dramatic days in malicious code history. This day saw the launch of the first virus outbreak to receive massive and daily cover-age in the mass media. This includes coverage on drivetime radio shows, in national and local newspapers, and on national and local television news shows. At one point, it was the lead story on the Peter Jennings ABC news broadcast.

During a congressional investigation of the incident, chairwoman Morella, a Republican from Maryland, said that the Love Bug virus was (to date) the fastest spreading and the most expensive computer virus in history. She noted that Lloyd's of London estimated the virus would cost more than $15 billion in damages.

The I Love You code was unique for its time because it was both a virus and a worm. According to an analysis of the timeline conducted by the GAO, the I Love You virus began replicating during business hours in the Far East, while the United States was sleeping. The Love Bug replicated with unprecedented speed throughout Asia and Europe. By 3 p.m. in Hong Kong, it was 9 a.m. in Western Europe, and the impact of the virus was becoming evident.

The Financial Services Information Sharing and Analysis Center (FS/ISAC) posted an alert to its members at approximately 3 a.m. EDT. At 5:45 a.m. EDT, a representative from private industry notified the National Infra-structure Protection Center (NIPC). The DoD Joint Task Force for Computer Network Defense (JTF-CND), which operates a 24-hour global operation cen-ter, was not alerted that the virus had hit the DoD at 6:40 a.m. EDT by one of the military services. Around 7:18 a.m. EDT, the Telecommunications Infor-mation Sharing and Analysis Center (T/ISAC) received a message that one of its major carriers was taking severe actions to close its e-mail gateways because of the I Love You virus.

At 7:45 a.m. EDT, two hours after it was first notified of the virus, the NIPC notified the Federal Computer Incident Response Center (FedCIRC) of the rapidly spreading virus, and FedCIRC began notifying senior agency officials via phone and fax. The NIPC would later be criticized for the lack of speed it exercised in responding to the incident. At 11:00 a.m. EDT, the NIPC posted a short alert paragraph on its home page warning about the I Love You virus. At about the same time, the CERT-CC sent an e-mail to the media stating that it had received more than 150 reports of the virus, but by that time it was too late.

The Love Bug usually came in the form of an e-mail message from someone the recipient knew, and it had an attachment called LOVE-LETTER-FOR-YOU.TXT.VBS. The attachment was a Visual Basic Script (VBS) file. If the recipients did not run the attached file, their systems were not affected, and they only needed to delete the e-mail and its attachment. However, when opened and the tasks ran, the malicious code would attempt to send copies of itself using Microsoft Outlook entries to everyone in the recipient's address book. It also attempted to infect the Internet relay chat (IRC) program so that the next time a user started chatting on the Internet, the worm could spread to everyone who connected to the chat server. The bug also searched for picture, video, and music files and would overwrite or replace them with a copy of itself. It also installed a password-stealing program that would become active when the recipient opened Internet Explorer 4 and rebooted the computer.

The Love Bug e-mail messages also began appearing with different subject lines, including Mother's Day, Joke, Very Funny, and VIRUS ALERT!!! The variants allowed the bug to bypass filters that may have been set up earlier to block I Love You messages. At least 14 different versions of the virus were identified. The GAO reported that in addition to hitting most federal agencies, the bug affected a wide variety of organizations, including AT&T, TWA, Ford Motor Company, the Washington Post, Dow Jones, ABC news, state governments, school systems, the International Monetary Fund, the British Parliament, Belgium's banking system, and credit unions.

One of the big lessons learned from the Love Bug was that there was a need for a coordinated and timely alert system for malicious code attacks. The NIPC, at that time, was the designated government agency to lead such efforts. The GAO noted that NIPC had some success, including in December 1999, when it posted warnings about a rash of denial-of-service attacks prominently on its Web site and offered a tool that could be downloaded to scan for the presence of the denial-of-service code. Two months later, the attack arrived in full force, compromising the services of Yahoo, eBay, and other Internet companies. However, the NIPC did not fare well during the Love Bug. It was important to understand where the process failed in the government, but it was also important to note that the process failed almost everywhere else as well. As the GAO noted, the NIPC first learned of the virus at 5:45 a.m. EDT. Over the next 2 hours, the NIPC checked other sources in attempts to verify the reports but had limited success. The NIPC contends that intelligence, defense, and law enforcement sources had produced no information, and only one reference was located in open sources.

It was not until 7:40 a.m. that two DoD sources notified the NIPC that the virus was spreading throughout the department's computer systems. That is when the NIPC notified the FedCIRC at GSA and CERT-CC. FedCIRC then undertook efforts to notify agency officials via fax and phone. This was too late. The GAO reported that only 2 of the 20 agencies interviewed stated that they first learned of the virus from FedCIRC. Twelve agencies first found out from their own users, three from vendors, two from news reports, and one from colleagues in Europe. The NIPC did not issue an alert about the Love Bug on its own Web page until 11 a.m., many hours after federal agencies were hit. This notice was a brief advisory, and the NIPC Web site did not provide advice on dealing with the virus until 10 p.m. that evening. The best way to describe the overall situation is that it was an ugly mess. The GAO highlighted the following for the United States Congress:

- For the most part, Federal agencies themselves responded promptly and appropriately once they learned about the virus. In some cases, however, getting the word out was difficult. At the DoD, for example, the lack of teleconferencing capability slowed the JTF-CND response because defense components had to be called individually.

- At the Department of Commerce (DoC), cleanup and containment efforts were delayed because many of the technical support staff had not yet arrived at work when users began reporting the virus.

- The National Aeronautics and Space Administration (NASA) also had difficulty communicating warnings when e-mail services disappeared. The Department of Justice (DoJ) officials also learned that the department needed better alternative methods for communicating when e-mail systems are down.

- Additionally, many agencies initially tried to filter out reception of the malicious I Love You messages. However, in doing so, some also filtered out e-mail alerts and communications regarding incident handling efforts that referred to the virus by name.

- Few federal components that either discovered or were alerted to the virus early effectively warned others. For example, the Treasury Department reported that the Customs Service received an Air Force Computer Emergency Response Team (AFCERT) advisory early on the morning of May 4, but that Customs did not share this information with other Treasury bureaus.

- The Department of Health and Human Services (HHS) was inundated with about 3 million malicious messages. Departmental components experienced disruptions in e-mail service ranging from a few hours to as many as six days, and department-wide e-mail communication capability was not fully restored until May 9. An HHS official observed that if a biologic outbreak had occurred simultaneously with the Love Bug infestation, the health and stability of the nation would have been compromised with the lack of computer network communication.

- At the DoD, enormous efforts were expended in containing and recovering from this virus. Military personnel from across the department were pulled from their primary responsibilities to assist. One DoD official noted that if such an attack were to occur over a substantial amount of time, reservists would have to be called for additional support. Some DoD machines required complete software reloads to overcome the extent of the damage.

- At least 1,000 files at NASA were damaged. Although some files were recovered from backup media, others were not.

- At the Department of Labor (DoL), recovery required more than 1,600 employee hours and more than 1,200 contractor hours.

- The Social Security Administration required five days to become fully functional and completely remove the virus from its systems.

- The Department of Energy (DoE) experienced a slowdown in external e-mail traffic, but suffered no disruption of mission-critical systems. Ten to 20 percent of DOE's computers nationwide required active cleanup.

- A vendor's 7:46 a.m. EDT warning to the Federal Emergency Management Agency (FEMA) enabled officials there to mitigate damage by restricting the packet size allowed through its firewalls until the necessary virus prevention software could be upgraded.

- As of May 10, the Veterans Health Administration (VHA) had received 7 million Love Bug messages, compared to a total of 750,000 received during the Melissa virus episode. The VHA spent about 240 staff hours to recover from the virus.

- Some of the Treasury Department's components required manual distribution of updated virus signature files because automated rollout systems for software updates were not in place.

- The Department of Agriculture (USDA) could not obtain the updated antivirus product it needed until after 1 p.m., in part because it had to compete with the vendor's other customers worldwide to obtain the updates.

The examples of pain, agony, and failure in government agencies during the Love Bug attack were well documented by the GAO. The events in the private sector have never been compiled as thoroughly, but some of the experiences noted by the author include the following:

- In Denver, Colorado, major businesses were at a standstill because the Love Bug crippled Microsoft Outlook, including e-mail, address books, and calendars. The common theme was that people did not know where they were supposed to be, and many did not have access to contact information that was trapped in their Outlook address books. The weather was good, and lots of people went to play golf.

- Many of the news reports focused on large business, state agencies, or school districts, but small to midsize businesses suffered great setbacks. One big problem was that smaller organizations often do not employ a full-time computer professional, so outside help was required. The backlog in service calls for many of the local computer service firms was at least days.

- The number of home-based computer users had been rising rapidly because of the general growth trends in Internet use. For many home

users, this was their first experience with a virus attack, and most had
no idea what they needed to do about it. Help lines for computer manufacturers and software vendors were clogged for days.

CODE RED(S)

On July 19, 2001, the Code Red virus infected more than 20,000 systems
within 10 minutes and more than 250,000 systems in just under 9 hours. An
estimated 975,000 infections occurred worldwide before Code Red subsided.
Code Red and Code Red II disrupted both government and business operations,
principally by slowing Internet service and forcing some organizations to disconnect from the Internet.

Code Red (named after a soft drink) used a denial-of-service attack to shut
down Web sites. The White House, which was the primary target of the denial-
of-service attack in the first version of Code Red, had to change the numerical
Internet address (IP address) of its Web site. The DoD shut down its public
Web sites, and the Treasury Department's Financial Management Service was
infected and had to be disconnected from the Internet.

Code Red worms also hit Microsoft's free e-mail service, Hotmail, caused
outages for users of Qwest's high-speed Internet service nationwide, and caused
delays in package deliveries by infecting systems belonging to FedEx. There
were also numerous reports of infections around the world.

The GAO analysis of the Code Red attack reported that it was more
sophisticated than those experienced in the past because the attack combined a
worm with a denial-of-service attack. Furthermore, with some reprogramming,
each variant of Code Red got smarter in terms of identifying vulnerable systems. Code Red II exploited the same vulnerability to spread itself as the original Code Red. However, instead of launching a denial-of-service attack against
a specific victim, it gives an attacker complete control over the infected system,
thereby letting the attacker perform any number of undesirable actions.

There were many lessons to be learned from the Code Red attack. First and
foremost was that thousands of systems operated by Microsoft's IIS Server had
not been updated with a patch that could have prevented Code Red as it was
originally written. Second, there were thousands of computers around the
world that nobody was paying any attention to. Staff in a data center in California that provided support for a hosting service reported that in the first two
hours of Code Red, they had more than 68,000 alarm messages from their net-

work monitoring system that a worm was scanning the Internet from computers housed in the data center.

The staff followed procedures that were established in the service agreements that governed their responsibilities in such a circumstance. E-mails were sent to several hundred companies that used e-commerce services provided by the hosting company. Dozens of the e-mails bounced back because the addresses were no longer valid. The companies using the e-commerce services did not respond to hundreds of other e-mails that may have reached their destination. Many contact telephone numbers were no longer in service. This went on for days as Code Red consumed vast quantities of bandwidth searching for new computers to infect.

The success of Code Red was largely a result of lax patch management and the fact that many organizations simply ignored requests from service providers to patch their systems. Unlike the Love Bug attack, the government provided considerable advanced warnings and urged owners and users to patch their systems. In this case it was clear that the government was on the case and people just ignored the warnings.

SIRCAM

SirCam was a malicious computer virus that spread primarily through e-mail. SirCam infected computers in more than 100 countries. It viciously replicated itself during the summer of 2001 before, during, and after the Code Red attacks. Once activated on an infected computer, SirCam searched through e-mails, user files, and e-mail address books to find new e-mail addresses to e-mail itself to in order to replicate. SirCam acted as stealware by e-mailing copies of files stored on the infected computer to unauthorized users. SirCam also attempted to delete files stored on hard drives or fill the remaining free space on the hard drive, making it impossible to perform common tasks such as saving files or printing.

According to a GAO analysis, SirCam reportedly caused considerable havoc. It was allegedly responsible for the leaking of secret documents from the government of Ukraine. It may also have been responsible for infecting computers at the FBI and sending some private, but not sensitive or classified, documents out in an e-mail. SirCam was much stealthier than the Melissa and I Love You viruses because it did not need to use the infected computer's e-mail program to replicate. SirCam came with its own internal capabilities to mail itself to other computers. SirCam could also spread through network connections in a Microsoft Windows network that had granted read-write access to the infected computer.

In general, SirCam was a far greater threat to the home PC user than Code Red and thus did not receive as much media attention as malicious code attacks that affected government organizations and large businesses. Many users reported getting hundreds of SirCam messages every day. This was especially true among users who had some sort of Web-based e-mail service or small businesses that had their e-mail addresses on their Web sites.

NIMDA

Nimda infections started on Tuesday, September 18, 2001, about 8:30 a.m. EDT. It took only a few hours for many organizations to be buried by the worm. The Nimda worm infected hundreds of thousands of computers around the world, using some of the most significant attack methods of Code Red II and Melissa. The infection period lasted several weeks, and many large organizations reported that Nimda had gotten behind their firewalls and was replicating within their networks.

Nimda modified Web files ending with .htm, .html, and .asp, as well as some other executable files found on the systems it infected. After doing so, it created numerous copies of itself under various file names. Nimda would then scan networks for vulnerable computers and replicate itself onto those computers in a never-ending process. Nimda also replicated itself through e-mail like a virus typically does. Nimda made it possible for infected computers to be used for attacks on Internet sites. Nimda also deliberately attacked computers that had been previously infected by Code Red if Code Red had not been removed from the computer. The worm-like replication process focused on searching out nearby computers on local networks.

SLAMMER

Many computer security experts called 2003 the Year of the Worm because for 12 months, worms spread across the Internet with the intensity of an apocalyptic event. It began in January, when the Slammer worm infected nearly 75,000 servers in 10 minutes. It was widely reported that Slammer clogged Bank of America's ATM network and caused sporadic flight delays for airlines.

On January 25, 2003, Slammer triggered a global Internet slowdown and caused considerable harm through network outages. The GAO reported that Slammer may have been responsible for impeding the operations of a 911 emergency call center as well as numerous canceled airline flights. In addition, the Nuclear Regulatory Commission reported that Slammer also infected a nuclear power plant's network, resulting in the inability of the computers to communicate with each other, disrupting two important systems at the facility. In July 2002, Microsoft had released a patch for its software vulnerability that was exploited by Slammer.

THE SUMMER OF 2003 BARRAGE OF BLASTER, SOBIG, AND MORE

In August, the worm Blaster, Welchia worm, Sobig, and their variants hit the Internet with severe force, spreading via e-mail and stealing addresses from infected computers. It replicated so fast that at one point, one out of every seventeen e-mail messages traveling through the Internet was a copy of Sobig. In China, the August onslaught may have affected 85 percent of Internet-connected computers. Sobig variants plagued the Internet for the remainder of 2003, replicating more than 1 million copies per month.

On August 11, 2003, the Blaster worm (also known as Lovsan) was launched. When the worm was successful, it caused the operating system of the infected computer to crash. Well before Blaster hit, the CERT/CC and other organizations advised of the vulnerability that could be exploited by a worm like Blaster. Again, many people did not heed the warning, and Blaster infected more than 120,000 unpatched computers during the first 36 hours of its release.

Within 24 hours, many computer users were experiencing lags and disruptions to their Internet service. The Maryland Motor Vehicle Administration was forced to shut down. Organizations around the world were starting to report problems. Blaster was programmed to launch a denial-of-service attack on Microsoft's Windows Update Web site (www.windowsupdate.com) on August 16. The Web site was where users could download security patches to ward off Blaster infections. Microsoft preempted the attack by disabling the Windows Update Web site.

The Blaster, which first appeared on August 11, did not require users to open e-mail attachments in order to spread. Instead, it propagated through a vulnerability in Microsoft software, infecting more than 1 million computers.

According to GAO analysis, two variants of the original Blaster worm were released on August 14. Federal agencies started to report problems associated with these worms to FedCIRC. On August 18, Welchia, a worm that exploited the same vulnerability as Blaster, was starting to replicate. Welchia affected several federal agencies, including components of the DoD and Veterans Affairs. Later reports came in from the Central Intelligence Agency (CIA), Environmental Protection Agency (EPA), the House of Representatives, and the USDA.

One malicious code writer who created a variant of Blaster, which infected more than 7,000 computers and tried to attack the Microsoft Web site, was apprehended by the FBI. Prosecutors alleged that a teenager modified the existing Blaster virus and unleashed his own more insidious version known as Blaster.B. A magistrate judge ordered that the teenager be subject to house arrest and denied access to the Internet. The DoJ, meanwhile, never caught the rest of the culprits in the August attack, but Homeland Security Secretary Tom Ridge issued a statement praising the arrest of the teenager.

One interesting dynamic that arose out of the August attacks was how universities dealt with students returning to school, many of whom had computers that were infected with the various worms and viruses. Major problems at several schools were reported by the media, including Oberlin College, the University of North Texas, Vanderbilt University, Salisbury University in Maryland, the Massachusetts Institute of Technology (MIT), the Palm Beach County public school district (the nation's 14th-largest school district), George Mason University, the University of Maryland, and the University of Virginia.

It seems that the computer-savvy under-twenties college students of the country were not very good at safe computing. Large percentages of students who brought their computers to school had viruses living on them. This resulted in double overtime for university networking staff, and some universities shut down their networks rather than risking infection.

EARLY 2004 WITH MYDOOM, NETSKY, AND MORE

In January 2004, just as the DHS launched its new centralized system to alert the country to threats to computer systems, a worm called MyDoom was wreaking havoc on thousands of Internet users. MyDoom disguised itself as e-mail that was not delivered properly as an attempt to get recipients to open attachments that launch the malicious code. Some organizations reported they were blocking more than 100,000 MyDoom-infected e-mails per hour. At another point, more than 40 percent of Internet traffic was comprised of MyDoom-infected e-mail messages. During its spread, MyDoom created hundreds of millions of e-mail messages.

In addition to clogging e-mail systems, MyDoom was programmed to use infected systems to launch a denial-of-service attack against the Web site of SCO Group Inc., a Utah company that claims to own the rights to some of the software code in Linux. The SCO Group offered a $250,000 bounty to anyone who was able to identify the creator or creators of the worm. One variant of MyDoom was programmed to prevent infected computers from viewing the Web sites of several virus protection software companies. MyDoom variants tended to avoid targeting e-mail addresses used by the government, military, and the search engine Google, as well as many domain names associated with the open-source software community.

MyDoom installed a backdoor on many computers that were infected. In another interesting twist, MyDoom also spread by attaching to downloads from a very popular file-sharing service, which lets Internet surfers share content such as games, movies, and music with each other for free. MyDoom won the honors for being the worst e-mail worm incident in virus history to date. There were three reasons behind the successful and speedy outbreak of MyDoom. Social engineering helped camouflage the worm by making it look like mail system error messages. Some of the infected attachments were also hidden inside ZIP files archives to make them less dangerous to users. The traffic created by MyDoom caused Web site performance to degrade as much as 50 percent.

By late February, more than a dozen bugs were replicating on the Internet, including multiple variants of Bagel, Netsky, and MyDoom, and a single variant of Hilton. On February 28, Central Command, an antivirus software and computer security firm, announced the discovery of three new variants of the Internet worm Bagel. Central Command concluded that this may indicate that the virus creator was attempting to get the worm to spread by challenging the ability of virus protection systems to adapt to detect his latest modifications.

ACTION STEPS TO COMBAT MALICIOUS CODE ATTACKS

The material in this chapter provides a historical overview of the malicious code that occurred over the last several years. As steps are taken to defend against malicious code attacks, managers, planners, trainers, and technical staff should understand what can happen during a malicious code attack and how that can affect organizations, including these basic concepts:

- Malicious code events can happen very quickly, which means organizations need to be constantly prepared to respond.

- Malicious code attacks can come in waves, and most viruses and worms are re-released in variant forms shortly after the original is released.

- Variants of viruses and worms are usually designed to overcome whatever defensive mechanism that was most recommended by software vendors or organizations like CERT/CC.

Organizations can take several steps to help reduce the impact of malicious code attacks. Recommended steps are included at the end of each chapter. The following action items are helpful in implementing developing training for employees about how malicious code attacks occur and the countermeasures that an organization has in place to deal with attacks. The action steps listed in Table 3-2 are designed to help an organization build knowledge on how to counter malicious code attacks.

Table 3.2 Action Steps to Combat Malicious Code Attacks

Number	Action Step
3.1	Assign a subcommittee of the working group to be responsible for developing and implementing an organization-wide training program on malicious code attacks.
3.2	Collect information about if and how the major malicious code events reviewed in this chapter have affected your organization.
3.3	Prepare material for use in training on how the major malicious code events reviewed in this chapter have affected your organization.
3.4	Prepare material for use in training on how your organization responded to the malicious code events reviewed in this chapter, and show how well the response helped your organization.

Table 3.2   Action Steps to Combat Malicious Code Attacks (continued)

Number	Action Step
3.5	Prepare material for use in training that explains how countermeasures and response plans in your organization have changed since the malicious code events reviewed in this chapter occurred.
3.6	Initiate a planning process for training development and delivery, including the designation of co-chairs for the training subcommittee.
3.7	Convene the training subcommittee for a launch and planning session.

4

Basic Steps to Combat Malicious Code Attacks

All organizations are vulnerable to malicious code attacks and need to take some steps to deploy countermeasures. This can sound overwhelming to some managers, especially those in small to midsize organizations and perhaps even those in large organizations that have resource constraints. However, not all countermeasures need to be complex. Some basic steps can be taken that can help dramatically reduce the impact of malicious code attacks. This chapter examines straightforward ways to accomplish these basic steps, including the following:

- Obtaining a better understanding of the risks
- Using security policies to set standards
- Managing system and patch updates
- Establishing a computer incident response team
- Training IT professionals
- Training end users
- Applying social engineering methods in an organization
- Working with law enforcement agencies

Keeping things simple is an insurmountable challenge for many people. When it comes to combating malicious code attacks, simplicity and focus can be an asset. There are probably some organizations where all computer security efforts are complex, including those that have material or data that a government has designated as classified, secret, top secret, or that requires protection under some other nomenclature. Organizations protecting systems that provide access to financial instruments and financial records also face greater challenges. Such organizations usually handle data that is protected by rather high standards that should already be in place.

It is, however, still advisable to consider these proposed methods and see if they can be applied to malicious code attack countermeasures. Most organizations do not face such complexity, and the steps outlined in this chapter may provide sufficient protection from most malicious code attacks.

UNDERSTANDING THE RISKS

Conducting a risk analysis can be an endlessly complicated project or a relatively straightforward task. You get to choose. A basic risk analysis identifies the risks to availability, integrity, and confidentiality. Figure 4-1 shows risk levels for computers and data. The three levels of risks that are the easiest to apply to computers, networking devices, and data are as follows:

- Low-risk systems are those computers or networking devices that if not available would have little impact on operations.

- Low-risk data is that which corrupted, manipulated, or viewed by unauthorized persons, would result in very little if any impact on your organization.

- Medium-risk systems are those computers or networking devices that if not available would have only moderate impact on operations and disrupt operations for just a few hours or days. Once the systems were running again, operations could be back on track in a short time.

- Medium-risk data is that which corrupted, manipulated, or viewed by unauthorized persons, would result in very little if only minor legal or financial ramifications for your organization. It would take little effort to restore the data.

- High-risk systems are those computers or networking devices that if not available would have an extreme impact on operations and disrupt operations for several days or longer. Once the systems were running again, it would take considerable time to get operations back on track.

- High-risk data is that which corrupted, manipulated, or viewed by unauthorized persons, would result in significant legal or financial

Risk Levels and Consequences	
Computer and Equipment	Data and Stored Information
High-Risk Level	
Lack of availability would have an extreme impact on operations.	Loss, corruption, or compromise would result in significant legal or financial consequences.
Medium-Risk Level	
Lack of availability would have a moderate impact on operations.	Loss, corruption, or compromise would result in very little legal or financial consequences.
Low-Risk Level	
Lack of availability would have little or no impact on operations.	Loss would have no legal or financial consequences.

Figure 4.1. *Risk Levels for Computers and Data*

ramifications for your organization. In addition, it would take significant effort to restore the data.

The first step in determining risk levels is to determine the systems and data that an organization relies on and that are the most important to operations and that may have legal or financial consequences if compromised. The larger an organization is, the more likely that there will be a sizable variance in the types of systems and data used. On the other hand, smaller organizations have far fewer systems, all of which may be important to operations.

Once the systems and data are identified, the next step in the risk analysis process is to determine how vulnerable the computers and networks are to malicious code attack or other types of intrusion. Several organizations can provide up to-date data on vulnerabilities, including CERT/CC (cert.org). You can get free e-mail updates on vulnerabilities from CERT/CC through the Department of Homeland Security (DHS) computer security updates (see dhs.gov).

To conduct the vulnerability assessment, you need to determine what types of software products are being used. This can be simplified. It is very likely that the desktop PCs in your organization are running Microsoft products. If so, then the systems are just as vulnerable as any system available. If your organization relies primarily on minicomputers, there may be fewer vulnerabilities, but even having a few vulnerabilities still means that security measures are necessary.

One of the traditional questions that risk assessments address is how likely is it that a malicious code attack would hit a specific organization. This has become a moot point. Random malicious code attacks are so prevalent that it is almost 100 percent certain that a computer without some level of protection would be infected in a very short time after connecting it to the Internet.

It is thus very likely that all organizations need virus protection software as well as firewalls or other access control systems. These two protection products will solve most malicious code–related problems. It is important, however, that systems are kept current and patches installed when possible. It is also important that systems are deployed with security-focused configurations. Manufacturers can provide information and employees can receive training on best configuration practices from several sources. There will be more discussion on these areas in subsequent chapters.

The main thing to remember about conducting risk assessments is to not do any more work than is necessary. All the risk assessments you can possibly perform will not eliminate the need for basic computer security products, configuration management, and patch management. Thus if your system mix is largely based on Microsoft products, your efforts may be better spent by making sure that you follow these basic security practices along with controlling system and data access so that only those employees who need access will get access.

USING SECURITY POLICIES TO SET STANDARDS

The Organization for Economic Cooperation and Development (OECD) is leading a global push for basic computer security measures. The OECD contends that every business should have a set of information security policies, standards, and procedures so that all employees know exactly what is expected of them. Security policies can be used to set standards for the installation, use, and maintenance of computer systems and networks. The list of possible policies can be lengthy. There are several sources from which to obtain model policies, procedures, or standards. One of the most popular is www.sans.org.

Most successful malicious code attacks are successful for simple reasons. The policies recommended here will eliminate many of the vulnerabilities and reduce much of the potential impact caused by attacks, as well as human error in dealing with attacks. The following types of policies should be included along with other policies in a written policy manual that governs the management of computer resources and the response to malicious code attacks:

- All computers must have recommended software for virus protection.

- Virus protection software must be updated regularly.

- Patches to eliminate software vulnerabilities must be installed as often as feasible.

- Each department must follow documented procedures to ensure the physical security of the computers and networking equipment.

- Each department must appoint, in writing, one or more information security officers (ISOs) to manage and administer department-level responsibility for information security and act as a liaison with the IT department and the computer incident response team.

- Each department must immediately assist the computer incident response team in the event of a security alert or incident.

- Every user must report all suspected viruses to the system administrator.

- All users must have unique user identifications (USERIDs) and personal (secret) passwords in order to access computers and networks.

- Records of USERIDs and user rights must be maintained for a period of two years from the date of employee termination, transfer, or other significant change in status.

- The computers and networks may only be used for activities specified in computer use and security policies.

- Network-connected workstations must always be logged off or secured when left unattended.

- No software may be introduced, installed, or used on computer resources without the express approval of the system administrator.

- All physical connections of computer systems to the organization network must be authorized in writing.

- System administrators must document the installation and use of software applications in conformity with all licensing agreements.

- Each employee must comply with procedures to safeguard against viruses and other harmful programs.

- Each department, division, or agency must perform data backups.

- Each department, division, or agency must train staff members in file recovery procedures.

- Computer users should not open e-mail attachments from unknown users.

- Computer users should not download any files from Web sites with which they are not familiar.

- Computer users should not have administrative rights to computers.

- Access to file and systems should only be granted to employees who work directly with the files or systems.

- All computer users should be trained on organization policies regarding computer usage as well as basic computer security measures.

SYSTEM AND PATCH UPDATES

More than 200 new vulnerabilities are discovered every month, which means that computers are frequently subject to attack. Effective patch management has become an essential computer security practice. IT management procedures and computer security procedures should address how patches are managed to meet the needs of an organization. Figure 4.2 shows the process of patch management.

It is important that responsibility for patch management is assigned to appropriate staff and that the staff is provided with the time and resources necessary to implement the required procedures. The number of people and other resources needed to accomplish this goal will obviously depend on the number of computers in an organization and the location of the computers. To facilitate the process of patch management, it is helpful to create and maintain a current inventory of all hardware equipment, software packages, services, and other technologies deployed in an organization. The inventory should indicate the type of system and the versions of each application software package installed, along with a patch history.

Various tools and services are available to assist in identifying vulnerabilities and their respective patches. Using multiple sources of information can help provide a more comprehensive view of vulnerabilities. When a vulnerability is

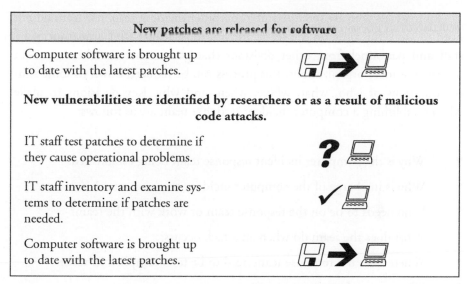

Figure 4.2. *Patch and Vulnerability Cycles*

published and a related patch and/or alternative workaround is released, appropriate action should be taken. The likelihood that the patch will disrupt computer systems must be considered, and patches should not be installed until they are tested. Computers connected to networks can be scanned using resource management software to determine which computer needs to be patched. If such software is used, then scanning should be done regularly. If automated approaches are not used, then IT personnel will need to manually check and update each computer. If this approach is used, an inventory of all of the computers in an organization that includes a patch history for each computer will make work go much faster and cost less money.

ESTABLISHING A COMPUTER INCIDENT RESPONSE TEAM

Experience has clearly shown that organizations need a response team, and that team needs to be in place and know what it is going to do before an attack occurs. Volumes have been written about how to establish a computer incident response team. Many computer security experts have contrived complex processes for establishing a computer incident response team, but for most organizations, these teams do not necessarily have to be large and complex. The number of computers and the number of locations at which an organization has computers will largely dictate the size of the response team.

Individuals who are members of a computer incident response team do not need to work full time on the team. In fact, most teams are formed out of IT staff and personnel from other divisions that go into action when an event occurs. For most organizations, this process can be reduced down to some simple questions of who, what, where, when, and why. Key decisions to make when establishing a computer incident response team are as follows:

- Why is the computer incident response team being established?
- Who is in charge of the computer incident response team?
- Who needs to be on the response team or work with the team?
- What does the team do when an attack occurs?
- Where does the response team need to be to accomplish its tasks?
- When must the team respond?

A computer incident response team can be established for several reasons, including dealing with malicious code attacks, responding to hacking incidents, or addressing problems involving digital intellectual property. All of these areas may require different skill sets, and different staff will need to work on the team. Almost all organizations need a response team to deal with malicious code attacks, but fewer organizations will need a team to deal with hacking incidents. For the purpose of this analysis, the focus is on establishing a computer incident response team to deal with malicious code attacks.

Deciding who is in charge of the computer incident response team depends on the size of the organization's IT staff. There should always be one person on the team who can work at the management level and be able to interact with other managers in the organization without problems. The management lead on the team in a small organization will likely be the MIS director. In larger organizations, it is most likely a functional area manager within the IT department.

There also needs to be a technical lead on the computer incident response team. This IT staff person will have knowledge of malicious code incidents, virus protection software, and the range of technical skills discussed in the following section on training for IT personnel. Other members of the team should be assigned as necessary. In larger organizations, the technical IT lead will need enough IT personnel to potentially visit every computer in the organization and perform an intervention by locating malicious code, eradicating it, and restoring computer operations.

In addition, a staff person from the public relations department or internal communications function could assist in communicating team needs throughout the organization. The best way to decide who needs to be on the team is to design a response process and figure out who will complete which tasks during the response. Establishing procedures for what the team does when an attack occurs will also help determine how many people and what type of people should be members of the team. The management lead and technical lead on the team should be able to develop the procedures.

Among the many things the team leads need to establish is where the response team needs to be located in order to accomplish its tasks and when the team must respond to an incident. These types of questions will vary considerably by the size, type, and geographic disbursement for computers in the organization.

TRAINING FOR IT PROFESSIONALS

Training for IT professionals is essential to effectively combat malicious code attacks. How an IT department is staffed will dictate many of the training needs. In addition to basic computer and network security skills, the IT staff members responsible for handling malicious code defense measures need knowledge in the following areas:

- Understanding the value of computer security and virus protection measures

- Knowing basic security management practices

- Installing, configuring, and deploying virus protection software selected by the organization

- Creating and implementing policies and alarms in security software

- Performing computer security software maintenance operations

- Performing administrative tasks required by the virus protection software selected by the organization

- Troubleshooting computer security and virus protection software problems

- Responding to a malicious code incident

- Working with other IT staff to improve computer security
- Training end users on virus protection methods
- Communicating with end users during a malicious code attack
- Preserving evidence for law enforcement of personnel actions
- Working with law enforcement on computer security incident investigations
- Monitoring emerging threats and obtaining vulnerability and patch information

Many sources of training can be helpful to improve response to malicious code attacks and computer security in general. Many junior colleges and community colleges are now offering short courses or semester-long courses on computer security and virus protection. The short courses are often one or two days in length and are relatively inexpensive. The semester-long courses require more commitment on the part of the person being trained, but they may also provide more in-depth learning experiences. There are also numerous organizations that provide training for specific operating systems, types of computers, and types of networking equipment. One of the most notable is SANS (www.sans.org). Note, however, that although SANS has an excellent reputation, course fees are considerably higher than those at local two-year schools.

Selecting which type of training is needed and the best source of training that will be helpful to an organization will depend on several factors, including how many staff members are in the IT department and how specialized those individuals are in their daily jobs. Many organizations have decided to have certified security personnel who have undergone extensive training and who have passed an examination to demonstrate their skill level. Smaller to midsize organizations probably do not require and cannot afford certified computer security staff. Large organizations tend to choose certified people because they can be assured of a minimum competency level.

TRAINING END USERS

Training end users is an important step in combating malicious code attacks. Many organizations now require employees to undergo basic training on computer security, virus protection measures, and organization policies covering the appropriate use of computers and software. Employees are also often required to take a brief test covering the major points in the training. In addition, employees are increasingly asked to sign statements that they have been trained on procedures and policies. These statements are usually kept in the individual personnel files of each employee.

A model training program for end users is provided in Chapter 8 of this book. The training program covers the following topics:

- Basic information about malicious code
- How to identify potentially malicious code
- What to do if there is suspect code
- What to expect from the IT department
- How the internal warning system works
- What to do if the organization is on alert

APPLYING SOCIAL ENGINEERING METHODS IN AN ORGANIZATION

Social engineering is one of the strongest weapons in the arsenals of hackers and malicious code writers. Social engineering is widely recognized to be the use of social disguises, cultural ploys, and psychological tricks to get employees of a company to assist hackers in their illegal intrusion or use of computer systems and networks. Social engineering is successful because most people are trusting and helpful toward individuals who approach their organizations seeking help. In addition, few organizations have trained their employees to identify social engineering efforts. The key to defending against socially engineered attacks is to socially engineer employees to be naturally impervious to the disguises, ploys, and tricks used by attackers. One way to achieve this goal is to teach employees to use their own social engineering abilities when dealing with every one they encounter.

The natural drive that most employees have of wanting to be helpful to others needs to be transformed. The emphasis needs to be shifted to where employees want to help those who should be helped and keep those who do not have authority to gain access to systems or information away from those systems. Employees can be trained to do this as a natural part of the helping process. What needs to get refocused about employees' behavior is how they set priorities on which gets helped first: the organization or the inquirer. There are several things to emphasize to employees that will decrease the likelihood that a socially engineered attack will succeed:

- Do not give information about computers, phone systems, or operational procedures to strangers or to anyone who is not specifically authorized to have access to that information.

- Always be suspicious of outside inquiries regardless of who people say they are, and verify the origin and purpose of all inquires.

- When in doubt, check with a supervisor before releasing any information.

WORKING WITH LAW ENFORCEMENT AGENCIES

Malicious code attacks can have numerous effects on computer systems and networks, including the installation of a Trojan or backdoor on your computer systems. These tactics let an intruder enter and take control of your computers. Sometimes these events involve disgruntled or recently terminated employees who understand an organization's computer systems and who can do considerably more damage than an outside attacker. In the event that you experience a crime against your computer systems, the FBI recommends that you do the following:

- *Respond quickly.* Contact law enforcement. Traces are often impossible to complete if too much time is wasted before alerting law enforcement or your own incident response team.

- *If unsure of what actions to take, DO NOT stop system processes or tamper with files.* This may destroy traces of intrusion.

- *Follow organizational policies and procedures.* Your organization should have a computer incident response capability and plan in place.

- *Use the telephone to communicate.* Attackers may be capable of monitoring e-mail traffic.

- *Contact the incident response team for your organization.* Quick technical expertise is crucial in preventing further damage and protecting potential evidence.

- *Establish points of contact with general counsel, emergency response staff, and law enforcement.* Preestablished contacts will help in a quick response effort.

- *Make copies of files an intruder may have altered or left.* If you have the technical expertise to copy files, this action will assist investigators as to when and how the intrusion may have occurred.

- *Identify a primary point of contact to handle potential evidence and establish a chain-of-custody for evidence.* Potential hardware and software evidence that is not properly controlled may lose its value.

- *DO NOT contact the suspected perpetrator.*

Compile as much information and data possible about the incident. Information that law enforcement investigators will find helpful includes the following:

- Date, time, and duration of incident

- The name, title, telephone number, fax number, and e-mail of the point of contact for law enforcement as well as the name of your organization, address, city, state, zip code, and country

- The physical locations of computer systems and or networks that have been compromised

- If the systems are managed in-house or by a contractor

- If the affected systems or networks are critical to the organization's mission

- The nature of the problem, which could include intrusion, system impairment, denial of resources, unauthorized root access, Web site defacement, compromise of system integrity, theft, or damage

- If the problem has been experienced before

- Suspected method of intrusion or attack, which could include a virus, exploited vulnerability, denial of service, distributed denial of service, backdoor, or Trojan horse

- The suspected perpetrators and the possible motivations of the attack, which could include an insider or disgruntled employee, former employee, or competitor (If the suspect is an employee or former employee, you should determine and report the type of system access the employee has or had.)

- An apparent source (IP address) of the intrusion or attack if known, and if there is any evidence of spoofing

- What computer system (hardware, operating system, or applications software) was affected

- What security infrastructure was in place, which could include an incident response team, encryption, firewall, secure remote access or authorization tools, intrusion detection system, security auditing tools, access control lists, or packet filtering

- If the intrusion or attack resulted in a loss or compromise of sensitive, classified, or proprietary information

- If the intrusion or attack resulted in damage to systems or data

- What actions have been taken to mitigate the intrusion or attack, which could include the system being disconnected from the network, system binaries checked, backup of affected systems, or log files examined

- What agencies have been contacted, which could include state or local police, CERT, or FedCIRC

- When was the last time your system was modified or updated, and the name of the company or organization that did the work (address, phone number, point of contact information)

It may also be necessary to determine a dollar value of damage, business loss, and cost to restore systems to normal operating conditions. The following information is helpful in determining dollar amounts:

- In the event that repairs or recovery were performed by a contractor, you should determine the charges incurred for services.

- If in-house staff were involved in determining the extent of the damage, repairing systems or data, and restoring systems to normal operating conditions, you should determine the number of hours staff expended to accomplish these tasks and the hourly wages, benefits, and overhead associated with each employee involved in the recovery.

- If business was disrupted in some way, you should determine the number of transactions or sales that were actually disrupted and their dollar value.

- If systems were impaired to the point that actual disrupted transactions or sales cannot be determined, then you should determine the dollar value of transactions or sales that occur on a comparable day for the duration of the system outage.

- If systems are used to produce goods, deliver services, or manage operations, then determine the value of that disruption. (You may have had similar experiences if operations were disrupted because of inclement weather, fires, earthquakes, or other disruptive incidents.)

- If systems were physically damaged, you need to know what you paid to acquire and install the systems.

- If systems were stolen, you need to know what you paid to acquire and install the systems and the cost of actions taken to ensure that information on the stolen systems cannot be used to access systems.

- If intellectual property or trade secrets were stolen, then you need to determine the value of that property.

- If intellectual property or trade secrets were used by a competitor or other party, then you need to determine the impact on your business.

ACTION STEPS TO COMBAT MALICIOUS CODE ATTACKS

The material in this chapter provides basic steps that most organizations can take to improve their resilience to counter malicious code attacks. As steps are taken to defend against malicious code attacks, managers, planners, trainers, and technical staff should understand how these basic steps contribute to the goal of countering malicious code attacks, including the following:

- How to conduct straightforward risk assessments of data, computer systems, and networks and how to identify vulnerabilities.

- How security policies can contribute to reducing the impact of malicious code attacks by setting standards for virus protection, computer security, patch management, and employee participation in identifying and responding to attacks.

- Having a computer incident response team that can go into action quickly can help reduce the impact of a malicious code attack by taking evasive action and restoring systems to normal operations as quickly as possible.

- Training end users is an important step in combating malicious code attacks because they will know how to report incidents and help the response team when necessary.

- Social engineering methods can be used to train employees on ways to do their jobs that reduce the possibility that a socially engineered attack is successful.

- It may be either necessary or helpful to work with law enforcement agencies under different circumstances, and the computer incident response team should be prepared to provide information to investigators.

Organizations can take several steps to help reduce the impact of malicious code attacks. Recommended steps are included at the end of each chapter. The following action items are helpful in implementing basic steps to reduce the impact of malicious code attacks. The action steps listed in Table 4-1 are designed to help an organization implement these steps.

Table 4.1   Action Steps to Combat Malicious Code Attacks

Number	Action Step
4.1	Develop a risk analysis for the organization for review by the work group. If an analysis was previously done, the malicious code work group should review that analysis and determine if it needs to be updated.
4.2	Review existing policies or develop new computer security policies that can help prevent malicious code attacks, applying the guidelines in this chapter.
4.3	Evaluate and modify system and patch update procedures to provide improved protection against malicious code attacks
4.4	Establish a team to respond to malicious code attacks.

Table 4.1   Action Steps to Combat Malicious Code Attacks (continued)

Number	Action Step
4.5	Evaluate the malicious code prevention training that IT staff have received and, if necessary, modify or expand training plans.
4.6	Have the training subcommittee review how social engineering methods can be applied in the training process for the organization.
4.7	Establish initial guidelines for when law enforcement agencies should be called about an incident and determine who in the organization should approve the action and who should make the call and act as liaison.

5
Organizing for Security, Prevention, and Response

Effectively responding to a malicious code attack in a manner that minimizes damage and disruption requires both speed and efficiency. The key ingredients to achieving a swift and efficient response are advance preparation and organization. The material in Chapter 4 explained the basic steps that organizations should take to be prepared to deal with malicious code attacks. This chapter builds on those steps by providing more details on budgeting, staffing, and product selection, including the following:

- Organization of the IT security function

- Where malicious code attack prevention fits into the IT security function

- Staffing for malicious code prevention in IT

- Budgeting for malicious code prevention

- Evaluating products for malicious code prevention

- Establishing and utilizing an alert system

- Establishing and utilizing a reporting system

- Corporate security and malicious code incident investigations

ORGANIZATION OF THE IT SECURITY FUNCTION

How an IT security function is staffed and the relationship between security staff and other IT personnel has evolved over the last three decades. Historically, the IT staff were responsible for password administration and monitoring network usage. Then the Internet came into widespread use. When it became clear that hackers and virus writers were using the Internet to wreak their own unique brand of havoc, most organizations assigned malicious code attack and hack attack prevention responsibilities to the IT security staff or the network management staff.

However, not all organizations can structure their IT security efforts in the same manner. There is often a lack of money and talent to approach IT security from the most idealized perspective. In organizations that have only a few IT staff members, the network administrator is often tasked with virus protection and network monitoring efforts. Patch management responsibilities in such organizations usually fall on the PC coordinators or PC technicians. When a malicious code incident occurs, the entire IT department is usually called on to respond. In large organizations, IT security specialists are often in their own work group within the IT department or the corporate security department.

The best way to organize an IT security function has been thoroughly thrashed about, but no definitive answer has emerged from the last decade of discussion. Of course this would be strongly debated by those who contend that their perspective is the best. Perhaps the best answer that can really be provided is that it depends. The follow-up question is of course "But on what does it depend?" Three basic conditions will highly influence IT security organization approaches:

1. Legal and regulatory requirements that an organization must comply with, such as banking companies and defense contractors

2. The type and source of applications software that an organization uses, including commercial off-the-shelf products, large and often expensive industry-specific products that can provide a range of support for certain types of organizations, and to what extent applications software was developed by in-house staff

3. The resources that are available for staffing and security tools

The conditions described previously can highly influence how many IT security staff members are required. These conditions also influence how IT security responsibilities may be distributed among other IT staff members. Table 5.1 shows some of the more popular IT security staffing alternatives.

Table 5.1   IT Security Function Staffing Alternatives

IT Security Function Alternatives	
Organization Characteristics	**IT Security Staffing Trends**
Heavy legal or statutory requirements	Several IT security specialists who ensure compliance with requirements
Reliance on commercial off-the-shelf microcomputer products	Few IT security specialists, with other IT staff performing security-related tasks for their areas
Industry-specific applications packages provide most of the automation support	Few, if any, IT security specialists, and software package provides access control functions
Primary applications developed in-house, which provide most of the automation support	Few, if any, IT security specialists, and software package provides access control functions

The best attitude managers can have toward establishing an IT security function is to do what works well for their organization. In some cases, shifts in the responsibilities of IT staff can help create an efficient security function. As previously discussed, training IT staff and end users is also an essential ingredient.

Managers should resist looking for an easy textbook answer to this challenge. Managers should also seek input from IT staff, legal counsel, public relations staff, and other key players in their organization when deciding the best approach toward staffing IT security. A well-thought-out approach will be far more effective in the long run. It is important to remember that overkill can be just as problematic as not allocating enough resources to the IT security and malicious code prevention efforts. A few guidelines to keep in mind when organizing an IT security function are as follows:

- Responsibilities for IT security need to be clearly stated in policies, procedures, and job descriptions.

- Adequate time and resources should be provided to dedicated IT security staff as well as other IT staff who have some level of responsibility for security.

- Standards for application development and deployment should encompass the security aspects of each type of application, and IT staff responsible for those applications should be trained to meet the standards.

WHERE MALICIOUS CODE ATTACK PREVENTION FITS INTO THE IT SECURITY FUNCTION

As the pervasiveness of computing continues to grow in breadth and scope, IT security is taking on many new dimensions. Bear in mind that malicious code attack prevention is only one aspect of IT security. The previously mentioned guidelines addressing responsibility for IT security also need to be applied to malicious code attack prevention within the larger realm of IT security, including the following:

- Responsibilities for malicious code attack prevention need to be clearly stated in policies, procedures, and job descriptions.

- Adequate time and resources should be provided to dedicated malicious code attack prevention staff as well as other IT staff who have some level of responsibility for dealing with malicious code attack prevention.

- Standards for technology deployment should encompass the malicious code attack prevention aspects of each type of technology, and IT staff responsible for the various types of technology should be trained to meet the standards.

The IT security function within the department, as well as responsibilities for malicious code attack prevention, are generally assigned to personnel at both the management and technical levels. Determining which management-level position in an IT department will have responsibility for IT security and malicious code attack prevention depends largely on the size and organizational structure of an IT department. Figure 5-1 shows an IT department organizational structure that has a division-level director of IT security. Figure 5-2 shows how other application- and location-specific security functions may be assigned to other division-level managers in the IT department.

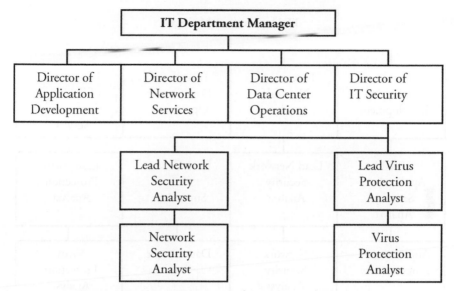

Figure 5.1. *Direct Reports to the Director of IT Security*

Most smaller to midsize organizations probably do not have a division-level director of IT security. Figure 5.3 shows how IT security responsibilities can be divided among other division-level managers. In this model the director of desktop computing services is responsible for malicious code attack prevention

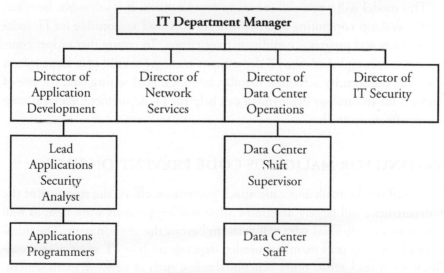

Figure 5.2. *IT Staff with Some Security Responsibility*

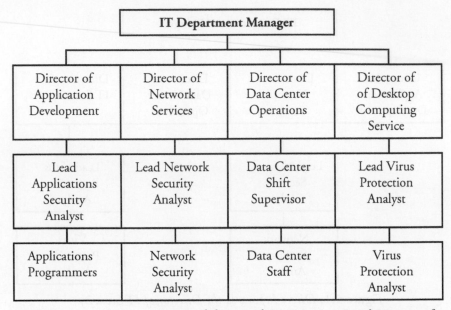

Figure 5.3. *IT Security Responsibilities with No Division-Level Director of IT Security*

and will probably handle virus prevention software products at the desktop level. The director of network services will most likely handle network-specific security functions.

This model will work well for many organizations. It is advisable, however, that the desktop computing and network services staff responsible for IT security products and programs coordinate their efforts. To ensure that proper coordination is accomplished, the IT department manager should play some role in overseeing the security activities. Regular meetings, goal setting, and the use of standards for technology deployment can help the IT department manager keep security efforts on track.

STAFFING FOR MALICIOUS CODE PREVENTION IN IT

When staffing the malicious code attack prevention effort, the structure of the IT department will largely determine what staffing patterns work best, as well as the type of individual who will perform best in the environment. The number of IT security staff members needed depends on how IT security responsibilities are spread across other functional areas, such as network management, applications development and maintenance, and desktop support.

If an organization has a staffing structure similar to what is described in Figure 5.1, which shows a structure that has a dedicated IT security director and dedicated security analysts, then it is likely that individuals who are trained and certified in security fields will be needed. On the other hand, if an organization has a staffing structure similar to what is described in Figure 5-3, which shows a structure where IT security functions are placed under functional area directors, then it is likely that the individuals responsible for security activities will need to perform other jobs. If this is the case, then those individuals will need to have multiple skill sets. This structure allows smaller IT departments to reduce costs because staff people can perform related tasks or other tasks that are necessary for the division to accomplish its mission.

During the last decade, average salaries for IT security staff have increased at a faster rate than for other IT professionals. During the last two years, the rate of increase has been only slightly higher than for other IT professionals. Several factors can contribute to this increase, including more IT professionals being trained in security and a downturn in the economy that resulted in extensive layoffs in IT-intensive organizations. Many IT professionals who were laid off or faced being without a job pursued training in IT security. Table 5-2 shows the average annual salaries for various IT security positions. The salaries were derived from a survey of advertised positions across the country that was conducted exclusively for this book.

Table 5.2   Annual Salaries for IT Security Staff

Position/Region	Average Annual Salary
IT Security Manager	
Midwest	$88,000
Northeast	$90,000
Southeast	$85,000
Southwest	$82,500
West	$96,000
U.S. average	$88,000

Table 5.2   Annual Salaries for IT Security Staff (continued)

IT Security Supervisor	
Midwest	$72,000
Northeast	$70,500
Southeast	$74,750
Southwest	$77,000
West	$66,000
U.S. average	$72,000
IT Security Analyst	
Midwest	$59,000
Northeast	$57,750
Southeast	$61,000
Southwest	$63,000
West	$54,000
U.S. average	$59,000
Network Security Analyst	
Midwest	$69,000
Northeast	$67,500
Southeast	$71,500
Southwest	$73,750
West	$63,500
U.S. average	$69,000
Web Security Analyst	
Midwest	$74,754
Northeast	$73,093
Southeast	$77,392
Southwest	$79,738
West	$68,524
U.S. average	$74,500

BUDGETING FOR MALICIOUS CODE PREVENTION

A focus group of IT managers and consultants was queried for this book about IT spending and IT security spending. Historically, organizations have spent between 2 to 3 percent of their annual revenue on IT, but organizations that are highly dependent on IT have spent as much as 7 percent of their annual revenue for IT. Typical spending for IT and network security has ranged from 2 to 5 percent of the annual IT budget. Tables 5.3, 5.4, and 5.5 show typical IT spending and IT security spending in low IT-dependent, medium IT-dependent, and high IT-dependent organizations, respectively.

Table 5.3   Spending Patterns in Low IT-Dependent Organizations

Annual Revenue	Annual IT Spending	Low IT Security Needs	High IT Security Needs
$10,000,000	$200,000	$4,000	$10,000
$25,000,000	$500,000	$10,000	$25,000
$50,000,000	$1,000,000	$20,000	$50,000
$100,000,000	$2,000,000	$40,000	$100,000
$250,000,000	$5,000,000	$100,000	$250,000
$500,000,000	$10,000,000	$200,000	$500,000

Table 5.4   Spending Patterns in Medium IT-Dependent Organizations

Annual Revenue	Annual IT Spending	Low IT Security Needs	High IT Security Needs
$10,000,000	$350,000	$7,000	$17,500
$25,000,000	$875,000	$17,500	$43,750
$50,000,000	$1,750,000	$35,000	$87,500
$100,000,000	$3,500,000	$70,000	$175,000
$250,000,000	$8,750,000	$175,000	$437,500
$500,000,000	$17,500,000	$350,000	$875,000

Table 5.5   Spending Patterns in High IT-Dependent Organizations

Annual Revenue	Annual IT Spending	Low IT Security Needs	High IT Security Needs
$10,000,000	$700,000	$14,000	$35,000
$25,000,000	$1,750,000	$35,000	$87,500
$50,000,000	$3,500,000	$70,000	$175,000
$100,000,000	$7,000,000	$140,000	$350,000
$250,000,000	$17,500,000	$350,000	$875,000
$500,000,000	$35,000,000	$700,000	$1,750,000

The annual spending on IT security shown in Tables 5.3, 5.4, and 5.5 usually reflects the cost of full-time equivalent staff assigned to security and any extraordinary spending for IT security that cannot be bundled in with a product or application. The cost of malicious code attack prevention products such as virus prevention and firewall software are most often included in the cost of desktop software or hardware or networking equipment, depending on where it is installed.

A survey of virus protection software prices conducted for this book showed that virus protection software could range from $35 to $85 per PC.

Table 5.6   Cost of Virus Prevention Software

Number of PCs	Annual Cost at $35 per PC	Annual Cost at $85 per PC
50	$1,750	$4,250
100	$3,500	$8,500
250	$8,750	$21,250
500	$17,500	$42,500
1,000	$35,000	$85,000
2,500	$87,500	$212,500
5,000	$175,000	$425,000

Table 5.7   Cost to Clean Computer of Malicious Code

Number of PCs	Virus Protection Software Annual Cost at $35 per PC	Cost to Clean Computer at $30 Per Incident			
		Cost to Clean up from One Incident Per Year	Cost to Clean up from Two Incidents Per Year	Cost to Clean up from Three Incidents Per Year	Cost to Clean up from Four Incidents Per Year
50	$1,750	$1,500	$3,000	$4,500	$6,000
100	$3,500	$3,000	$6,000	$9,000	$12,000
250	$8,750	$7,500	$15,000	$22,500	$30,000
500	$17,500	$15,000	$30,000	$45,000	$60,000
1000	$35,000	$30,000	$60,000	$90,000	$120,000
2500	$87,500	$75,000	$150,000	$225,000	$300,000
5000	$175,000	$150,000	$300,000	$450,000	$600,000

The cost per PC depends on the volume of licenses purchased, the type of software, the type of support, and the type of service offerings that an organization purchases from a brand-name virus protection software company. Table 5.6 shows the annual cost of virus protection software at the two price points for organizations with 50 to 5,000 PCs.

Virus prevention software products are an incredible bargain considering how much money they can save when compared to the cost of recovering from a malicious code attack. In 2003, five or six viruses or worms replicated themselves rapidly. Table 5-7 shows the cost of cleaning computers from one, two, three, and four malicious code incidents in a period of one year at $30 per machine. The cost of cleaning malicious code from PCs for two widespread incidents is more than the cost of spending $35 per year for virus protection software per machine each year. Table 5.8 shows that at the same cleaning cost per machine, the cost of spending $85 per year per machine for virus protection software is recovered if three incidents are avoided.

Table 5.8   Cost to Clean Computer of Malicious Code

Number of PCs	Virus Protection Software Annual Cost at $85 per PC	Cost to Clean Computer at $30 Per Incident			
		Cost to Clean up from One Incident Per Year	Cost to Clean up from Two Incidents Per Year	Cost to Clean up from Three Incidents Per Year	Cost to Clean up from Four Incidents Per Year
50	$4,250	$1,500	$3,000	$4,500	$6,000
100	$8,500	$3,000	$6,000	$9,000	$12,000
250	$21,250	$7,500	$15,000	$22,500	$30,000
500	$42,500	$15,000	$30,000	$45,000	$60,000
1000	$85,000	$30,000	$60,000	$90,000	$120,000
2500	$212,500	$75,000	$150,000	$225,000	$300,000
5000	$425,000	$150,000	$300,000	$450,000	$600,000

EVALUATING PRODUCTS FOR MALICIOUS CODE PREVENTION

There are two major product groups from which organizations need to select protection tools. Virus prevention software, or antivirus software as it is often called, is a must-have product. Keep in mind that many Internet service providers (ISPs) are now cleaning files of malicious code when those files pass through their networks, so organizations should consider using an ISP that provides these services. Firewall products are also necessary for systems that are connected to the Internet through any type of connection.

The process of evaluating malicious code prevention products has become far easier over the last two years. Recognize that virus protection software producers are cooperative and exchange a considerable amount of information about viruses and other forms of malicious code. Software products from the major companies in the virus protection arena certainly differ, but they all have a high level of effectiveness. Accepting this point brings up the need to consider what kind of service and support the different companies offer and how that may help meet the needs of your organization.

Please note that the major software providers offer similar types of service packages. The virus protection and firewall software companies would certainly debate this assertion, but after reviewing their Web sites, you will find that although the language and presentation differ, the services are remarkably similar. In addition to similar software and services, the prices for basic products are also similar. On a per-desktop basis, packages can cost as little as $20 per year and can reach a high of $100 per year. A study of product costs found two clusters of price points, with an average low cluster price of around $35 per year and an average high cluster price of $85 per year. Service and support packages, which include alerts and automated script and database updates, are described differently from company to company, but ultimately you can get the same support from all of the major companies.

So where then is the decision point? The best thing to do is to look inside your organization and examine how virus protection and firewall products are being managed. Are things going well or are there problems? Depending on what you conclude about the status of malicious code protection in your organization, it is possible that one of the virus protection software companies may appeal to you more than the others. It is advisable not to make product selection a panic point in your efforts to protect your organization form malicious code attacks. No matter which product you pick, if your organization is not managing updates for the virus protection software and implementing policies and procedures presented in other parts of this book, you will fail to protect your organization.

Software products alone will not solve your problem, but the proper deployment and management of a brand-name virus protection software package combined with good patch management, security-conscious computer user procedures, and adequate staff training will protect you from most malicious code incidents. Before picking a product, you should install it and learn how the product works. You should examine how the interfaces work and if they are comfortable for your staff. Also decide if the help files and alerts are formatted in a manner that allows your staff to get the most out of the products and services provided by the vendor.

ESTABLISHING AND UTILIZING AN ALERT SYSTEM

A malicious code attack alert system has several functions. The primary function is to notify IT personnel who have some responsibility for combating malicious code attacks that a new virus or worm is in the wild or that an attack

The Malicious Code Attack Alert System
Alert of active threat information is received through warnings from virus protection companies or other sources. 
Internal systems notify computer incident response team members. 
Computer incident response team evaluates the threat and vulnerabilities of the organization. 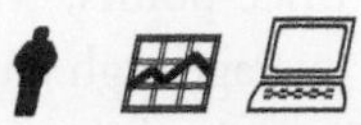
Computer incident response team starts to deploy updates to virus protection software and patches to computers. 
Computer incident response team notifies management and computer users of possible threat. 
Computer incident response team monitors threat situation for virus or worm variants. 
If attacks continue, computer incident response team deploys additional updates to virus protection software and patches to computers. 

Figure 5.4. *How Malicious Code Attack Alert Systems Can Work*

has commenced on the organization's computers. These alerts prompt activation of the computer incident response team. Figure 5.4 shows how a malicious code attack alert system can work and how the computer incident response team reacts.

The computer incident response team can be alerted through several sources. Many organizations have some form of service package with their virus protection software company that provides alerts via e-mail or other means. Other organizations rely on bulletins from government-supported services such as CERT/CC. In many instances, the computer incident response team is alerted by a computer user within the organization or through an alarm message from the virus protection software that is installed on computers or e-mail servers.

Another function of the alert system within an organization is to notify computer users that a new threat is present or an attack is in progress. This aspect of the alert process is helpful because computer users will be aware of what types of e-mail messages or computer behaviors they should be on the lookout for and should report to the computer incident response team.

Alerts to computer users are usually distributed through the organization's e-mail system. However, under emergency circumstances, some organizations have used their public broadcast system or have distributed brightly colored flyers at the reception desk, gates, or entranceways. Such alerts should provide a description of the virus or worm, an explanation of what can happen if systems are infected, and what computer users should do if they suspect they have been infected. This type of notification process helps mobilize employees to be an effective part of the countermeasures. This approach can also help the computer response team make quick interventions when malicious code starts infecting computers.

ESTABLISHING AND UTILIZING A REPORTING SYSTEM

An internal reporting system for malicious code incidents allows employees, customers, and associates to report things they know or suspect to be malicious code. Such reporting systems are an excellent way to catch malicious code attacks before they get out of control. There are several elements to a successful internal reporting system:

- Employee training to identify malicious or suspect code

- A process for employees to send or file reports

- A process for IT staff to receive reports and respond

A model training program for computer users in an organization is provided in Chapter 8. It is important to implement such training programs because employees can become the first line of defense in the fight against malicious code attacks. As mentioned in previous chapters, training is especially important to fight against socially engineered attacks.

The IT department, in combination with other contributing divisions or work groups in an organization, need to work together to design, launch, and support an internal reporting system. The system needs to be easy to use, employees need to be informed about the system and trained to use it, and above all the system must be responsive. If employees do not believe that the IT department is responding to reports and taking them seriously, the system will quickly deteriorate and cease to function.

One of the easiest ways to support the reporting system is through the help desk or other function that is the major point of contact employees have with the IT department. The help desk staff need to be trained to receive the reports and make first-level interventions. If help desk staff cannot resolve the issue, a member of the computer incident response team should be responsible for investigating, identifying if an actual problem exists, and responding as quickly as possible in a manner that halts the attack.

It is advisable to have multiple ways for an employee to file a report. E-mail or a Web-based form are good options, but they will not work if the employee's computer is not functioning. This means that a telephone contact option should also be available. The key to success in all of the contact systems is to make sure that e-mails, Web-based reports, and voice-mail systems are checked frequently enough to enable a rapid response.

CORPORATE SECURITY AND MALICIOUS CODE INCIDENT INVESTIGATIONS

Responding to and eradicating a malicious code attack is essential for managing countermeasures. However, it is also important that attacks be investigated and a report be compiled that can be used as a feedback mechanism into the countermeasures system. In most cases, random e-mail viruses and worms that are in the wild are just that: They are moving about the Internet and landing wherever they can. But it is important to be reasonably sure that an incident is random in order to determine that an individual or group of attackers has not singled out the organization as a target.

An incident investigation and report should cover many of the points that would be important to report to law enforcement agencies, which were covered in Chapter 4. However, several areas should be covered that may not be of interest to law enforcement agencies; thus it is strongly recommended that two separate reporting approaches be developed. An internal investigation should cover the following areas:

•   When the incident began and how long it lasted

- How the malicious code ended up in the organization's systems
- Which systems were affected
- What the impact of the attack was in terms of downtime or disruption
- Which vulnerabilities were exploited
- If the same problem has occurred before and, if so, when
- How the computer incident response team became aware of the incident
- How the incident was resolved
- Whether existing procedures were adequate or require modification
- If vulnerabilities were eliminated
- How vulnerabilities were eliminated
- What, if any, new lessons were learned from the incident
- What, if any, procedures should be changed as a result of the incident

The management lead and technical lead responsible for malicious code attack countermeasures should review each report for potential actions. The reports should also be reviewed by other IT managers who are responsible for areas that may be vulnerable or where procedures may need to be changed in order to prevent similar incidents in the future.

ACTION STEPS TO COMBAT MALICIOUS CODE ATTACKS

The material in this chapter provides several points for evaluating or improving the malicious code protection activities of an organization. This chapter builds on the basic steps described in Chapter 4 by providing more details on budgeting, staffing, and product. As steps are taken to defend against malicious code attacks, managers, planners, trainers, and technical staff should understand how the management of IT security efforts contributes to the goal of having effective countermeasures to malicious code attacks, including the following:

- There are several viable approaches to organizing staff and responsibilities for malicious code attack prevention.

- It is important to adequately staff malicious code attack prevention efforts and train IT personnel on product usage as well as an organization's policies and procedures.

- Leading malicious code attack prevention software companies offer similar products and services, but a specific offering may better meet the needs of an organization more so than others.

- Reporting processes for potential attacks and alert systems that prompt the actions of a computer incident response team are an important element of effective countermeasures against malicious code attacks.

- Investigations of malicious code attacks should be used to determine the source of the attack as well as to evaluate the effectiveness of response efforts.

Organizations can take several steps to help reduce the impact of malicious code attacks. Recommended steps are included at the end of each chapter. The action steps listed in Table 5.9 are designed to help an organization with action items that are helpful in organizing IT security efforts.

Table 5.9   Action Steps to Combat Malicious Code Attacks

Number	Action Step
5.1	Evaluate how IT security functions are structured in your organization, and determine if changes would improve security or better utilize limited resources.
5.2	Evaluate how malicious code attack prevention efforts are supported in your organization, and determine if changes would improve protection or better utilize limited resources.
5.3	Evaluate how malicious code attack prevention efforts are staffed in your organization, and determine if more people need to be trained to support the efforts.
5.4	Review the budget for malicious code attack prevention products and staff in your organization, and determine if spending more money would actually improve protection efforts.

Table 5.9   Action Steps to Combat Malicious Code Attacks (continued)

Number	Action Step
5.5	Once the other evaluations are completed, review the malicious code protection products that are used in your organization, and determine if changing products or expanding service contracts with your vendor would actually improve protection efforts.
5.6	Evaluate the alert system in your organization and determine if it is adequate to bring the computer incident response team into action quickly enough and if it notifies computer users in a timely manner to ensure that they can contribute to incident response rather than cause an incident to get worse.
5.7	Evaluate the system that allows users to report problems to the computer incident response team in a manner that helps facilitate speedy and efficient response to potential malicious code attacks.
5.8	Evaluate the process by which malicious code incidents are investigated in your organization, and determine if the process is adequate or if changes would actually improve protection efforts.
5.9	The malicious code work group should review all of the evaluations and make recommendations to the appropriate managers or IT security staff.

6
Controlling Computer Behavior of Employees

There are two major weaknesses that all organizations have in their efforts to combat malicious code attacks: technology and computer users. We have discussed the necessity of setting and adhering to standards for computer system configuration and the deployment of defensive software, including virus protection packages and firewalls. In Chapter 8, a model training program is provided to teach computer users how to identify potential attacks and how to work with the computer incident response team.

The social and cultural patterns of computer users are certainly fascinating to those who are working to increase productivity through automation and to power their organization through the deployment of business solutions. However, the social and cultural patterns of computer users also creates one of the major weaknesses in efforts to combat malicious code attacks.

End users—you can't live without them and you can't live with them! Such is the sentiment of many IT professionals who have had to work long hours cleaning up after an attack that occurred because a computer user opened an e-mail attachment from an unknown sender or visited a non-work-related Web site that was infected with a worm.

Training end users is essential to defend against malicious code attacks. Teaching computer users about socially engineered efforts that attackers use is also helpful. But many organizations have decided that those efforts alone are not sufficient. This chapter presents several techniques that organizations can employ to supplement other efforts when developing malicious code attack countermeasures, including the following:

- Policies on appropriate use of corporate systems
- Monitoring employee behavior

- Web site blockers and Internet filters

- Cookie spyware blockers

- Pop-up blockers

- Controlling downloads

- SPAM control

POLICIES ON APPROPRIATE USE OF CORPORATE SYSTEMS

Many employees may view restrictions on how they can use computers and networks as a punitive measure. Others have argued about the legality and ethics of monitoring or controlling employee behavior. Both of those discussions are endless circles that may never be resolved. There are security reasons why employees' use of computers and networks needs to be controlled. Malicious code attacks of all sorts can originate through e-mail usage, visits to Web sites, SPAM, and many other nasty things that circulate on the Internet. The main goal of malicious code countermeasures is to stop attacks. If controlling the way in which employees use computers and networks can reduce the frequency and severity of attacks, then organizations should take reasonable steps to do so.

There are two major perspectives about the appropriate use of computer equipment, telephone systems, and other assets of an organization. The most rigid approach is to take a position that everything belongs to the organization and employees are not allowed to do anything personal within the confines of the facilities or with any equipment or systems. Dumb! Really dumb! This approach is extremely impractical when it comes to motivating employees, supporting a family-friendly work environment, or dealing with the many issues that are created by a work-oriented society that demands dedication, long hours, and high productivity from employees.

A more realistic approach has been adopted by many organizations, including several government agencies—limited personal use. This means that activity that is conducted for purposes other than accomplishing official or otherwise authorized activities and that does not adversely affect the employee's job performance is acceptable within a set of guidelines. The first principle of limited personal use is that such use has a negligible impact on the organization and the performance of employees, which means that the impact is sufficiently small that the quantity or cost may be disregarded.

The second principle encompasses what is called nonduty time, that is the time when an employee is not expected to be performing official business. This could be characterized as an employee's own off-duty hours such as before or after a workday, lunch periods, authorized breaks, or weekends or holidays. The third principle of limited personal use is that such use does not violate any contractual agreements, local or federal laws, and regulations that an organization is required to adhere to because of the nature of the business activity that is performed or supported.

Applying these principles to the use of computer systems and networks does require that an organization think through the consequences of social and cultural behaviors of employees and examine which of those behaviors could create problems or increase the possibility of a malicious attack against systems. Examples of acceptable and unacceptable behaviors are shown in Table 6.1.

Table 6.1   Do's and Don'ts of Personal Computer Use

Acceptable	NOT Acceptable
Use of the Internet during nonduty time	Loading personally owned software onto computers
Use of e-mail for professional communications not directly related to an immediate task or project	Use of an organization's postage systems, color copiers, or other technologies with high associated costs
Participation in professional e-mail lists, listservs, and discussion groups	Transmitting or receiving large attachments though e-mail
Use of computer software packages for professional activities	Use of broadcast transmissions, or mass mailings
Use of laser printers for small print tasks	Downloading copyright-protected material
Use of the Internet for educational purposes	Use of long-distance phone services or 900 numbers
Short-duration phone calls for personal or family matters (relevant when data communications and telecommunications systems are integrated)	Visiting Internet sites that contain materials that are violent, threatening, racially or sexually harassing, or that otherwise violate laws

Many attorneys recommend that organizations clearly communicate the acceptable-use policies to employees both in writing and in a formal training program. Employees should be trained on the policies and be required to sign a statement that they have received the training and will adhere to the employer's policies on acceptable use of computer systems and networks.

MONITORING EMPLOYEE BEHAVIOR

Monitoring employee use of computers, e-mail systems, and Internet habits has been a rather controversial activity during the last decade. Interviews conducted with IT security managers for this book showed that most organizations do not have an extensive monitoring program in place. Other organizations do monitor Internet use, including the movement of large files attached to e-mail messages.

The attorneys interviewed for this book generally concurred that monitoring employee behavior can yield both mixed results and potential legal hassles. There was a rather unanimous urging that if monitoring is to be done, employees should be informed of monitoring policies and be asked to sign a statement that they have been informed and will comply with acceptable-use policies. It is advisable that before you start using any of these tools to monitor employees' behavior, you consult with your attorney about local or state laws.

Monitoring and scanning e-mail, along with monitoring Internet usage, are the two most common forms of monitoring employee behavior performed by organizations. Scanning e-mails with the intent of blocking SPAM is covered later in this chapter. The same software that can be used to block employees from visiting particular Web sites or types of Web sites can provide a means to monitor surfing behavior or attempted Web surfing behavior. These utilities can track all Web surfing behavior, including the use of Web-based shopping sites, hobby sites, and Web sites that contain violent or unacceptable content. These tools are discussed later in this chapter.

There are also several software packages available known as *keyloggers*, which record every keystroke made on a computer on every window, even on password-protected boxes. The software can start up whenever a computer starts up and record everything being typed, e-mails, messages, documents, Web pages, usernames, and passwords. Keyloggers can be installed and run on the computers of all employees or only on selected employees. Figure 6.1 illustrates how keyloggers are used to monitor employees.

How Keyloggers Are Used to Monitor Employees

Keylogger software is installed on computers.

Employees use computers for daily tasks.

Keylogger records everything being typed, e-mails, messages, documents, Web pages, and stores data in a file.

Supervisors or IT staff review contents of files to determine what users did on their computers.

Supervisors or IT staff monitor trends in employee computer use.

Employees are counseled for their inappropriate computer use if necessary.

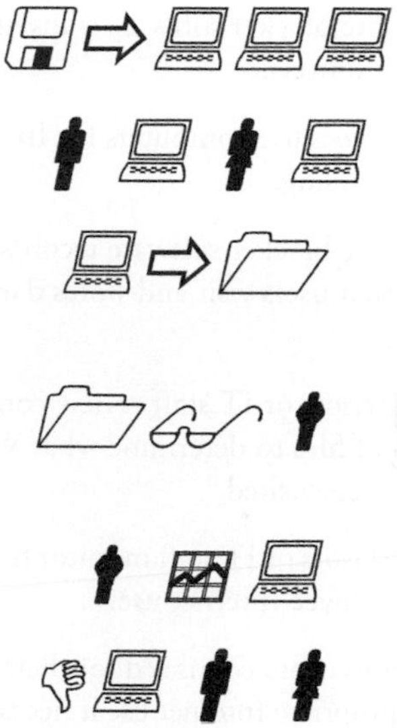

Figure 6.1. *How Keyloggers Are Used to Monitor Employees*

WEB SITE BLOCKERS AND INTERNET FILTERS

There are several good reasons to block certain types of Web sites. Pornography Web sites, for example, are notorious for planting Web bugs on the computers of people who visit the sites. Other types of sites have been blamed for spreading worms and viruses, including many Web sites in Russia and China. Still other Web sites have been known to collect information about visitors by placing spyware on their computers and then selling that information to marketing companies. Many organizations have had problems with employees visiting pornographic Web sites during working hours. There have been situations where this behavior has resulted in sexual harassment lawsuits being filed by female employees.

Although there are many good reasons to use Web site blockers, there can also be unintended consequences for using blocking software. One of the more famous incidents involved blocking Web sites that had the word *breast* on any of the pages. This resulted in dozens of Web sites offering information about breast cancer being blocked.

How Web Site Blockers Monitor Internet Use

Web site blocker software is installed on computers.	
Employees use computers for Internet browsing.	
Web site blocker software records sites that users visit and stores data in a file.	
Supervisors or IT staff review contents of files to determine what Web sites users visited.	
Supervisors or IT staff monitor trends in employee Internet use.	
Employees are counseled for their inappropriate Internet use if necessary.	

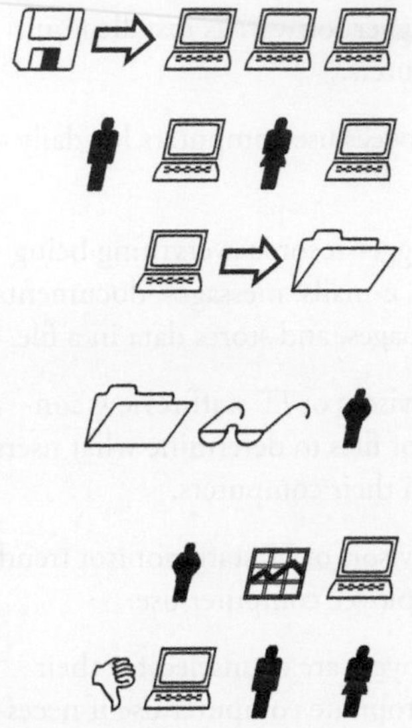

Figure 6.2. *How Web Site Blockers Monitor Internet Use*

The technology that supports the popular Web site blockers and Internet filters that parents use to keep their kids from visiting inappropriate Web sites, such as those offering pornographic images, has found its way into many organizations. Web site blocking software is relatively inexpensive and can be installed on a computer for as little as $30 per year. Bear in mind, however, that installation and maintenance does require staff time, which can drive up the per-computer costs rather dramatically. Figure 6.2 shows how Web site blockers monitor Internet use, and Figure 6.3 shows how Web site blockers stop visits to sites.

Web site blockers allow system administrators to block Web sites in several ways, including the following:

- Setting blocking preferences on specific categories
- Blocking Web sites by creating a list of allowed or blocked sites
- Checking for offensive text-based words and phrases

The Internet usage patterns of employees can be tracked and recorded in an event log, which keeps a list of Web sites that each user visited or attempted to

How Web Site Blockers Stop Visits to Sites

Web site blocker software is installed on computers.	
Employees use computers for Internet browsing.	
Web site blocker software checks the Web site the user wants to visit against list and conditions in a file.	
If the Web site is acceptable, the blocking software allows the user to view.	
If the Web site is not acceptable, the blocking software disallows the user to view.	

Figure 6.3. *How Web Site Blockers Stop Visits to Sites*

visit. This information can be reviewed by supervisors or IT staff. Web site blocking software packages offer several features that make administration easier and less time consuming, including the following:

- Filters and lists can be updated automatically on a subscription basis.

- Supervisors or other designated personnel can be authorized to override blocked Web sites.

- Administration functions and responsibilities can be delegated and assigned.

- Many products have an easy-to-use, Web-based interface.

- Administrators can create custom categories of Web sites to be blocked.

- Filters can be set for specific users or groups just like file access is set.

- Filters can be set to be turned off or on based on a schedule for times of the day or days of the week.

- Blocking functions can be set to a monitor-only mode and provide a warning to users about the appropriateness of the Web site they are visiting.

- Some products support several languages, including English, French, Italian, Spanish, Danish, Swedish, German, Dutch, Portuguese, and Japanese.

Web site blockers and content filters generally provide administrators with a wide variety of reports to analyze Web surfing activities and e-mail usage. Reports can be provided in a format that can be viewed on a computer screen or printed. Administrators can use preconfigured reports or customize their own reports. Some products allow reports to be produced on demand, or administrators can be scheduled to run reports during off-peak hours and then the reports can be e-mailed to designated recipients in various file formats. The content of reports can include the following items:

- AOL Chat Rooms and IRC chat usage
- AOL Instant Messenger, MSN Instant Messenger, and Yahoo Messenger usage
- Attachments that are viewed or opened
- Bandwidth consumption by user or time of day
- Blocked activities by category or with extensive detail
- Blocked connections
- Filtering categories by user or time of day
- Filtering modes by user or time of day
- FTP requests and session details
- Hotmail, Yahoo e-mail, AOL Internet e-mail, NetZero Web-based e-mail, ATT Worldnet Web-based e-mail, and Netscape Web-based e-mail usage
- KaAaA and KaAaA Lite, Gnucleus, Limewire, and other peer-to-peer system usage
- Microsoft Exchange usage
- Most active users
- Most popular file types, FTP sites, newsgroups, and secure Web sites
- Names of all files downloaded using peer-to-peer systems

- Newsgroup participation
- Reports for usage by individuals, departments, or other groups
- SMTP/POP3 e-mail usage
- Specific URLs visited
- Text of all searches conducted within peer-to-peer systems
- Top sites requested by user or time of day
- Top 10 blocked users
- Total number of visits to specific Web sites
- Visits to secure Web sites

COOKIE AND SPYWARE BLOCKERS

The most widely used monitoring tool on the World Wide Web is the cookie. A cookie is a small file that generally holds some unique identifying information. When computer users visit cookie-powered Web sites, a cookie file or several cookie files are downloaded into the cache of the Web browser. The cookie identifies the computer user to the Web site during each visit.

Cookies were designed to help computer users by saving them time when they visited Web sites that require registration or a login process. The Web site developer also benefited by being able to serve the visitor faster and track the frequency of visits and the preferences that a user has in browsing, shopping, or researching. The Web site is able to match the visitor with profile information stored on a server. Examples of benefits for both the user and an e-commerce site are functions like speedy checkout or quick purchasing. The visitor saves time and the Web site saves resources by not having to serve up numerous pages to get an order for merchandise processed.

The Federal Trade Commission (FTC) is working rather vigorously to make sure that companies keep the promises they make to Web site users about privacy protection and the precautions they take to secure that information. Many Web sites post privacy policies that describe how a Web site visitor's information is collected, used, shared, and secured. Using its authority under Section 5 of the FTC Act, which prohibits unfair or deceptive practices, the FTC has brought several cases to enforce the promises made in privacy statements, including promises about the security of information.

Many Web marketing companies utilize cookies to bring targeted advertising methods to cyberspace. These cookies can be identified by every Web site that uses the services of the marketing company, and data can be collected over a period of time to create a profile of individual Internet users. This allows Web sites to selectively display banners for products or services that the visitor had expressed interest in during visits to various Web sites. Cookie-blocking software packages provide a variety of functions, including the following:

- The ability to add servers and cookies to a file and designating them as always accept, accept for session-only, or reject

- Automatically being able to accept or reject cookies received from unspecified servers without user interaction based on designation or expiration date

- Automatically being able to accept or reject certain types of cookies without user interaction

- Maintenance of a list of the cookies accepted and rejected from all servers for current sessions

- Classification of cookies already stored on the computer

In addition to cookies, several types of invasive parasitic programs are designed to install and maintain themselves on a computer without the permission of the computer user. These include Web bugs, spyware spybots, adware, malware, browser hijackers, and keyloggers. Web bugs are often unseen graphic files that load with a Web page. Once installed, they can track activities and gather information about computer usage and send that information back to a server someplace on the Internet.

Several symptoms indicate that a computer may have been infected with parasitic code, including an unusually slow Internet connection, the computer freezing or hanging, frequent system crashes, boot-up taking an usually long time, or an unusual level of bandwidth usage. In addition, unauthorized Web sites may have added an icon to the desktop or added themselves to the browser's list of favorite Internet Web sites. Antivirus and firewall protection is often bypassed by parasitic software because many of these programs are small and stealthy. In addition, manual removal is often difficult for computer users who do not have technical skills.

Several software products are available on the market to protect computers against parasitic code. The annual cost for these products ranges from $30 to $50. Bear in mind, as with all protective products, that staff time will be required to install and maintain the software. The functionality of anti-invasive software products can include the following features:

- Automatic review and removal of all various forms of parasitic software
- Automatic updates of the software with new threat detection profiles
- Detection and removal of registry entries made by parasitic software
- Interception of parasitic file downloads
- Monitoring and logging of parasitic software that tries to install on computers
- Quarantine of infected or suspicious files
- Removal of objects or modules that hijack Internet browsers
- System scanning to detect parasitic software

POP-UP BLOCKERS

Web browser poppers, known as pop-ups, popexits, and popunders, are considered by many computer users to be absolute Internet pollution. Network managers and planners see them as something that has little value and that consumes bandwidth and thus resources. Web marketers, on the other hand, view these popping browser windows as a potential source of revenue.

Major media Web sites, as well as many search engines, hit site visitors with a new browser popper every time they click on a link to navigate through the Web site. Some Web sites now have poppers that appear when a mouse moves across a certain area of a Web page. The poppers usually open new browser windows that take time to close and are irritating to manage when browsing the World Wide Web.

Several IT security managers have expressed concern about the future of browser poppers. These concerns are mostly focused on the possibility of poppers introducing new vulnerabilities during Web surfing. Other concerns include having some sort of active code that will stay in a browser cache after the computer user is finished surfing. Several IT security managers contend that it will not take long for malicious code attackers to start taking advantage of how poppers work and use them to launch new types of attacks.

Popper stoppers provide a variety of functions, including keeping new browser windows from opening or the browser window from being resized when a new window is opened. In addition, an icon can be set to blink when a popper has been blocked, which informs computer users that they are at a site that uses browser poppers. Some popper blockers have the capability of adding toolbars to the browser interface. Popper stoppers can now also be made to act selectively when users create a list of Web sites from which they will accept poppers. The latest editions of popper stoppers can also halt script-driven ads that are created in FLASH or other animation software.

CONTROLLING DOWNLOADS

The Internet provides access to literally millions of files that can be downloaded. These include software, text files, PDF files, music and video files, movies, photographic images, and many more. Many Web sites also offer free downloads, and numerous Web sites are home to pirated material that Internet users can access. The rise in popularity of celebrity streaming media clips in the workplace has resulted in companies experiencing slow Internet connections for work-related Internet use, clogged bandwidth, and a loss in employee productivity. According to Websense, 44 percent of corporate employees use streaming media at the office.

According to a March 2003 peer-to-peer (P2P) study conducted by Palisade Systems, file-sharing applications have no legitimate value in the workplace. Since the emergence of Napster in 2000, file-sharing applications have become more sophisticated. The Gnutella file-sharing applications, such as Morpheus, LimeWire, and BearShare, make it possible to trade virtually any file on a user's computer where the P2P software resides. Palisade Systems monitored a file-sharing network for nearly three weeks and discovered the following:

- 42 percent of all requests were for adult or child pornography.

- 38 percent of all requests were for copyrighted audio files.

- 73 percent of all movie searches were for pornography

- 24 percent of all image searches were for child pornography.

- 6 percent of all searches were for child pornography of some kind.

- Only 3 percent of searches were for nonpornographic or noncopyrighted materials.

- 97 percent of all activities on a P2P network could result in a criminal or civil suit against a business for copyright infringement, sexual harassment, or felony-level offenses.

Palisade Systems found that in addition to criminal and civil liability risks, there are network security risks associated with P2P, including the following:

- *Accidental sharing of sensitive files.* Confidential business and personal files may be shared with other P2P users. Unknowingly, the user grants access to multiple folders or the entire hard drive containing these files.

- *Releasing viruses and trojans.* Files are most often from unknown users. Music files or executable program files exchanged on a P2P network can contain viruses or Trojans. The files can circumvent most e-mail or Web download antivirus solutions, and the viruses are discovered after damage has been done.

- *Installation of spyware.* Applications such as KaZaA and BearShare require users to install spyware on their computers as part of the licensing agreement. Spyware tracks the activities of the user and reports them to a third-party organization.

- *Bandwidth clogging.* A few users downloading movies or large files can easily clog an organization's network, halting business-critical operations on the network.

Many organizations are starting to block downloads from P2P servers, including files from the following:

Ares	BearShare	BitTorrent
Blubster	DC++	DirectConnect
Earthstation 5	EDonkey	EMule
FastTrack	Filetopia	Gnucleus
Gnutella	Grokster	IMesh

KaZaA	KaZaA Lite	LimeWire
Morpheus	MP2P	Mute
OpenNap	Overnet	Piolet
RockitNet	Shareaza	Soribada
Waste	WinMX	XoloX

Many organizations are also starting to block downloads with certain types of files extensions that are known to be dangerous and potentially destructive, including the following:

.asd	.asf	.asx
.bas	.bat	.chm
.cmd	.com	.dll
.exe	.hlp	.hta
.hto	.js	.jse
.link	.lnk	.pif
.reg	.scr	.vb
.vbe	.vbs	.wsc
.wsf	.wsh	

To deal with some of the problems associated with downloading, many organizations do not assign administrator rights on computers to employees. This keeps individual employees from installing software downloaded from the Internet or designed to work in P2P networks. Whenever someone in the organization needs to receive a specific attachment having one of the extensions listed previously, the receiver asks the sender to change the file's extension. This helps confirm that a known person has sent the attachment. Another tactic that network administrators take to discourage downloading files is to slow down access to selected or filtered sites. By deliberately slowing down access, users can be discouraged from browsing nonbusiness or objectionable sites or trying to download files.

SPAM CONTROL

SPAM consumes network and computing resources, occupies mail administrator and help desk personnel time, and reduces worker productivity because it takes time for e-mail users to sort through and delete unwanted or unsolicited messages. In some cases, SPAM messages have been known to contain some sort of malicious code that infects systems and requires cleanup. The costs of SPAM to computer users have been increasing with the megagrowth in the number of SPAM messages circulating on the Internet.

The network and computing resources to deal with SPAM messages include a slowdown in networks by increasing the traffic load and consuming more storage space on e-mail servers as well as the consumption of bandwidth. Other concerns that organizations have about SPAM is that some messages act as spyware or stealware, using a variety of techniques to harvest e-mail addresses from the computers of recipients. The economic impacts of SPAM can be categorized in several ways, including the following:

- Productivity loss from employees dealing with SPAM

- Additional costs for network and computing resources

- Additional human resources required to deploy technology to deal with SPAM

- Security risks caused by SPAM attacks, such as e-mail–transported viruses and worms

- Finally, many people are now concerned that there may be potential legal liability if SPAM hijacks an e-mail system to replicate and send itself to listings in a computer user's e-mail address book.

If an e-mail server has an open relay, someone could access it and pass SPAM through it. And if your proxy server is open, a spammer could use it to connect to your mail server and send bulk e-mail anonymously. As the FTC points out, not only can these abuses overload your server, but the spammer could also damage your organization's reputation because it will appear that your system sent the SPAM. There are many reasons why you do not want this to happen.

The Securities and Exchange Commission (SEC) points out that the Internet is an excellent tool for fraudsters. Many fraudsters use SPAM newsletters to offer their so-called independent research, and their newsletters masquerade as sources of unbiased information, when in fact they stand to profit handsomely if they convince investors to buy or sell particular stocks. Some e-mail newsletters falsely claim to independently research the stocks they profile. Others spread false information or promote worthless stocks. The most notorious sometimes scalp the stocks they hype, driving up the price of the stock with their baseless recommendations and then selling their own holdings at high prices and high profits.

Fraudsters also use SPAM to draw people to their online bulletin boards, which have become an increasingly popular forum for investors to share information. These bulletin boards typically feature threads made up of numerous messages on various investment opportunities. Although some messages may be true, many turn out to be bogus or even scams. Fraudsters often pump up a company or pretend to reveal inside information about upcoming announcements, new products, or lucrative contracts.

Because SPAM is so cheap and easy to create, fraudsters increasingly use it to find investors for bogus investment schemes or to spread false information about a company. Spam allows the unscrupulous to target many more potential investors than cold calling or mass mailing. Using a bulk e-mail program, spammers can send personalized messages to thousands and even millions of Internet users at a time.

The types of investment fraud seen online mirror the frauds perpetrated over the phone or through the mail. Remember that fraudsters can use a variety of Internet tools to spread false information, including bulletin boards, online newsletters, SPAM, or chat (including Internet relay chat or Web page chat). They can also build a glitzy, sophisticated Web page. All of these tools cost very little money and can be found at the fingertips of fraudsters.

There are millions of messages sent everyday that read: "How To Make Big Money From Your Home Computer!!!" One online promoter claimed that investors could "Turn $5 into $60,000 in just three to six weeks." In reality, this program was nothing more than an electronic version of the classic pyramid scheme in which participants attempt to make money solely by recruiting new participants into the program.

The SEC actively investigates allegations of Internet investment fraud and, in many cases, has taken quick action to stop scams. The SEC has also coordinated with federal and state criminal authorities to put Internet fraudsters in jail. Here is a sampling of recent cases in which the SEC took action to fight Internet fraud:

- Francis A. Tribble and Sloane Fitzgerald, Inc. sent more than 6 million unsolicited e-mails, built bogus Web sites, and distributed an online newsletter over a 10-month period to promote two small, thinly traded microcap companies. Because they failed to tell investors that the companies they were touting had agreed to pay them in cash and securities, the SEC sued both Tribble and Sloane to stop them from violating the law again and imposed a $15,000 penalty on Tribble. Their massive spamming campaign triggered the largest number of complaints to the SEC's online Enforcement Complaint Center.

- Charles O. Huttoe and 12 other defendants secretly distributed to friends and family nearly 42 million shares of Systems of Excellence, Inc., known by its ticker symbol SEXI. Huttoe drove up the price of SEXI shares through false press releases claiming multimillion-dollar sales that did not exist, an acquisition that had not occurred, and revenue projections that had no basis in reality. He also bribed co-defendant SGA Goldstar to tout SEXI to subscribers of SGA Goldstar's online Whisper Stocks newsletter. The SEC obtained court orders freezing Huttoe's assets and those of various others who participated in the scheme or who received fraud proceeds. Six people, including Huttoe and Theodore R. Melcher, Jr., the author of the online newsletter, were also convicted of criminal violations. Both Huttoe and Melcher were sentenced to federal prison. The SEC has thus far recovered approximately $11 million in illegal profits from the various defendants.

- Matthew Bowin recruited investors for his company, Interactive Products and Services, in a direct public offering done entirely over the Internet. He raised $190,000 from 150 investors. But instead of using the money to build the company, Bowin pocketed the proceeds and bought groceries and stereo equipment. The SEC sued Bowin in a civil case, and the Santa Cruz, California District Attorney's Office prosecuted him criminally. He was convicted of 54 felony counts and sentenced to 10 years in jail.

- IVT Systems solicited investments to finance the construction of an ethanol plant in the Dominican Republic. The Internet solicitations promised a return of 50 percent or more with no reasonable basis for the prediction. Their literature contained lies about contracts with well-known companies and omitted other important information for investors. After the SEC filed a complaint, they agreed to stop breaking the law.

- Gene Block and Renate Haag were caught offering prime bank securities, a type of security that doesn't even exist. They collected more than $3.5 million by promising to double investors' money in four months. The SEC has frozen their assets and stopped them from continuing their fraud.

- Daniel Odulo was stopped from soliciting investors for a proposed eel farm. Odulo promised investors a whopping 20 percent return, claiming that the investment was low risk. When he was caught by the SEC, he consented to the court order stopping him from breaking the securities laws.

Technology to stop SPAM is offered by several companies, many of which offer other security products such as virus protection software. When selecting SPAM-filtering products, the principles and steps for evaluating security tools described in Chapter 5 should be applied. SPAM-blocking software packages use several methods to detect, isolate, and otherwise stop SPAM, including the following:

- *Examination of the e-mail message header, layout, and organization to identify SPAM characteristics and attributes*, which enables a pattern-matching scheme that can apply specifically designed algorithms to determine the probability that a message is SPAM

- *Heuristic detection*, which applies a series of tests to determine if a message is SPAM

- *Blacklists*, which allow IT staff to block e-mail from known spammers

- *Whitelists*, which allow messages to be received from designated e-mail addresses

- *Content filtering*, which checks for keywords or phrases that appear in an e-mail message

- *Quarantining*, which allows IT staff to route messages to different holding servers for later examination

ACTION STEPS TO COMBAT MALICIOUS CODE ATTACKS

The material in this chapter focuses on ways to help control the computer usage patterns of employees in a manner that can help counter malicious code attacks. As steps are taken to defend against malicious code attacks, managers, planners, trainers, and technical staff should understand how these methods contribute to countering malicious code attacks, including the following:

- The benefits and problems associated with monitoring employee computer use

- How Web site blockers work and how they can help counter malicious code attacks

- How cookie and popper blockers work and how they can help counter malicious code attacks

- How blocking certain file downloads can help counter malicious code attacks

- How to select and deploy SPAM-blocking technology to help counter malicious code attacks

Organizations can take several steps to help reduce the impact of malicious code attacks. Recommended steps are included at the end of each chapter. The action steps listed in Table 6.2 are designed to help provide an organization with action items that are helpful in organizing IT security efforts.

Table 6.2   Action Steps to Combat Malicious Code Attacks

Number	Action Step
6.1	Evaluate if and how employee computer use should be monitored to help reduce the possibility of malicious code attacks.

Table 6.2   Action Steps to Combat Malicious Code Attacks (continued)

Number	Action Step
6.2	Evaluate if and how Web site blockers or content filters should be used to help reduce the possibility of malicious code attacks.
6.3	Evaluate if and how cookie blockers should be used to help reduce the possibility of malicious code attacks.
6.4	Evaluate if and how popper blockers should be used to help reduce the possibility of malicious code attacks.
6.5	Evaluate if and how blocking certain types of file downloads should be used to help reduce the possibility of malicious code attacks.
6.6	Evaluate the impact of SPAM in your organization, and determine if SPAM countermeasures are adequate or should be modified with SPAM-blocking technology to help reduce the possibility of malicious code attacks.
6.7	The work group should meet to determine action on each of these evaluations and make recommendations to the appropriate managers.

7

Responding to a Malicious Code Incident

When responding to a malicious code attack, a lot can be learned about the state of technology, the level of training that IT staff and users have in dealing with an attack, and the politics and personalities inside an organization. A learning organization will use the results of every incident with which the computer incident response team deals as a feedback mechanism to improve defenses as well as response procedures.

The steps taken during a computer incident response can happen quickly and can overlap in their sequence. There is a general flow of events, but that flow can be disrupted or the response team may have to loop back to previous steps if several variants of a malicious code attack in a rapid sequence. As we have learned during the last several years, several worms or viruses can also be simultaneously active. To help illustrate how a computer incident response unfolds, a case study is presented and the response log is completed for all of the steps in the process, including the following:

- First report
- Confirmation process
- Mobilizing the response team
- Notifying management
- Using an alert system and informing end users about the attack
- Cleanup and restoration
- Controlling and capturing malicious code
- Identifying the source of malicious code

- Preserving evidence
- When to call law enforcement
- Enterprise-wide eradication
- Return to normal operations
- Analyzing lessons learned

The case study used to illustrate how the computer incident response process works shows how a small company of 240 people was infected by a malicious code attack and the basic steps that were taken by the response team. The case also shows how the team worked with the CEO's office and how various resources were leveraged throughout the organization to respond to the attack. The response to the incident spans a three-day period.

Many organizations maintain a log of all of the events that occur and the steps that the response team takes. The first things on the log of an actual event will include the following information:

- When the first report was received
- How the first report was received
- Who performed the confirmation of the attack
- The nature of the malicious code attack
- When the computer incident response team was mobilized
- Who is leading the team and who is on the team

ABOUT THE CASE STUDY

James Heartfield founded Heartfield Enterprises, an engineering firm of 240 employees, in 1958. The company had grown slowly and steadily through the cold war and the space race. Many of the engineers, all specialists in their fields, had once worked for larger companies in the defense industry or for the U.S. government.

The organization structure of the firm was traditionally very flat. James Heartfield ran the company more like a think tank or a university department than a for-profit enterprise. Several labs operated independently, and before his death, James Heartfield ran the company like a grandfather instead of a CEO.

The labs were accustomed to their autonomy. Each lab had its own equipment and its own computers. About the only thing that was shared among the labs was a local area network (LAN), which was installed in the mid-1990s to provide Internet access throughout the facility and replace redundant slower connections with high-speed access and reduce connectivity costs in the process.

Tonya Heartfield, the 34-year-old granddaughter of James Heartfield, now runs the company. After he died, his wife, his daughter (Tonya's mother), and an invalid son inherited all of James' wealth along with the company. Tonya was the only one in the family capable of running the company. She had worked there since she was a child and had attended college, earning a Ph.D. in chemical engineering with a specialty in materials science. Tonya was slowly bringing a more structured management style to the company. This included the centralization of enterprise services, including human resource management, purchasing, facilities management, information technology, and telecommunications management. As you may suspect, not everybody in Heartfield Enterprises was happy with Tonya's approach.

Before the central LAN was installed and a firewall put into place, the individual labs were almost constantly plagued with virus and hack attacks. Even before she took over as the CEO and president, Tonya had been working to improve computer security, but the company would still be crippled by a malicious code attack once or twice a year. Her grandfather had resisted spending money on security or, for that matter, spending enough money to have an IT staff in place.

With the help of her advisor, Brandon L. Harris, Tonya had created an IT department of six people. They had been working for a few months trying to improve security, get a consistent patch management program in place across the company, and train computer users on security issues. They had also been working to get a computer-based HR management system, a browser-based purchasing system, and other management tools in place. Tonya's goal was to bring more order to the company and to better control overhead costs.

On May 1st, Heartfield Enterprises was hit with a worm that was infecting systems worldwide. The newly hired IT staff had worked to update operating system software and antivirus software on computers throughout the organization. Many departments were resisting the centralization efforts and would not let the new IT staff work on their computers. The new IT staff had been preparing for this attack for several weeks. They had hoped to get more computers patched and protected, but time had run out. Tonya Heartfield and B. Simons, the new IT director, had already decided that if an attack came before they were finished with their work, they would try to maintain Internet connectivity as long as possible. Most of the employees had become very dependent on the Internet, and Tonya did not want to penalize those who had cooperated with her efforts by cutting off access. B. Simons had warned her that this could be a tricky situation but agreed with the strategy.

When MayDay hit Heartfield Enterprises, the computer incident response team found several obstacles to their efforts, including these issues:

- A lack of documentation on network design and configuration
- Numerous desktop computers that had not been patched for a long period
- Outdated antivirus software on many computers
- Several computers without any antivirus software
- An incomplete inventory of all computers in the organization
- A lack of cooperation from departments in assisting in the defense.
- A lack of cooperation from end users, who would not let the response team work on their computers
- A Trojan on three computers that was moving files from the organization while MayDay was attacking
- Delays in determining who worked on the computers that had an active Trojan moving files
- User IDs and passwords that were used by former employees for which access had not been disabled
- Uncertainty on how to deal with law enforcement during an investigation of the Trojan and file theft

THE FIRST REPORT OF A MALICIOUS CODE ATTACK

Computer incident response begins with a first report of a malicious code attack. The first report can come from a variety of sources. The most likely sources are computer users or IT security personnel who monitor traffic or alarms that are raised by automated monitors installed on a network. In some cases, a user may report what he or she suspects may be a virus or worm. This could end up being a single occurrence or a false alarm or the start of an onslaught of infections. In other cases, IT security personnel will observe worms that attempt to penetrate a network and fail or can witness a massive attack that results in widespread infections.

The frequency of attack attempts and the frequency of end user reports will help determine if a real problem is occurring. IT security staff who act quickly can often keep sporadic occurrences from becoming major incidents. They can also identify a major outbreak as it begins and quickly patch systems or bolster defenses to prevent large-scale disruptions. Computer incident log entries from the case study relating to the first report phase of an incident are shown in Table 7.1.

Table 7.1   Log Entries for First Report

Date/ Time	Log Entry	Staff
May 1 6:45 a.m.	CEO had computer problems. She reported to help desk via voice mail.	TG
7:10 a.m.	Network manager received reports from CERT/CC of MayDay worm on home computer before coming to work.	TG
7:16 a.m.	Network manager notified IT staff and CEO's office of expected problems via PDA alert system.	TG
7:30 a.m.	Four different employees had left messages on the help desk answering machine stating they had problems and thought it may be a virus.	RR
7:35 a.m.	Two calls are received from employees by LC while she was driving to work. The users reported they thought they had a virus.	LC

THE CONFIRMATION PROCESS

When the frequency of intrusion attempts or actual incidents that affect servers or desktop computers escalates, it is probably time for a full-scale computer incident response. IT security personnel use a variety of sources to confirm that a high-level threat is underway. This includes information from antivirus software companies and CERT/CC. Reports from end users help confirm that the computers in an organization are vulnerable and that an attack is in progress.

The confirmation process is not extremely complicated, but before an entire computer incident response team is mobilized and IT staff are pulled from other tasks to initiate a response, it is advisable that the scope and potential magnitude of a threat is properly assessed. Using a combination of external reports and internal identifications of a malicious code, the IT staff responsible for confirmation can mobilize the response team.

The confirmation process helps set an agenda for response. Once an attack is confirmed and the threat is assessed, the response team begins to implement procedures necessary to counter an attack and secure the computing environ-

Table 7.2   Log Entries for Confirmation Process

Date/ Time	Log Entry	Staff
May 1 7:45 a.m.	Positive identification was made of the worm infecting systems. It is the worm in the CERT/CC bulletin of 6:00 a.m. on May 1.	TG
7:47 a.m.	We compared several samples of the malicious code that infected some of the computers at HE, and it appears at this point that there is only one active worm.	TG
7:55 a.m.	Analysis of computer system inventories indicates that as many as 50% of the systems could be infected by this worm. Those are the systems that have not been updated with patches and new antivirus software.	FR
7:55 a.m.	Additional reports have been received from end users indicating that infections at HE are becoming widespread.	TG

ment. Once this is achieved, the computer incident response team will follow procedures similar to those described in the rest of this chapter. Computer incident log entries from the case study relating to the confirmation phase of an incident are shown in Table 7.2.

MOBILIZING THE RESPONSE TEAM

The practical consequences for mobilizing the computer incident response team will vary by organization and will depend on how the team is staffed. Generally speaking, the IT security staff, network administration personnel, help desk staff, and appropriate IT managers are involved in a response. In a company as small as Heartfield Enterprises, the computer incident response team ends up being the entire IT department.

If procedures that have been recommended in prior chapters of this book have been developed, the members of the computer incident response team will have been identified. The IT staff person responsible for confirmation and initiating mobilization will know whom to call. Computer incident log entries from the case study relating to the mobilization phase of an incident are shown in Table 7.3.

Table 7.3   Log Entries for Mobilization

Date/ Time	Log Entry	Staff
May 1 8:00 a.m.	The computer incident response team is mobilized. TG is team lead. FR is network control and monitoring. LC, LK, and RR are on the desktop and end user team.	TG
8:04 a.m.	Desktop teams were dispatched to find out more about infections on desktops in various departments.	TG
8:05 a.m.	IT manager B. Simons went to discuss the incident with the CEO's office.	TG
8:06 a.m.	FR is starting to work on blocking traffic at the gateway and isolating infected systems from the internal network.	TG

NOTIFYING MANAGEMENT

It is important that organization managers at all levels understand when a computer incident is in progress. Managers can help inform end users about the attack and ease workflow problems that may result from the attack. Many organizations have a management notification procedure in place. The means or notification needs to be customized for an organization and should take advantage of existing communications mechanisms. Notifications to management should be straightforward and nontechnical. They should also include an estimate of the magnitude of the expected problem as well as an expected duration of the problem. Computer incident log entries from the case study relating to the notification of management about an incident are shown in Table 7.4.

Table 7.4   Log Entries for Notification of Management

Date/ Time	Log Entry	Staff
May 1 8:10 a.m.	IT manager B. Simons met with the CEO and her staff to discuss the incident and internal communications.	TG
8:15 a.m.	The CEO's office staff has been assigned to work on alerting departments and employees.	TG
8:16 a.m.	The CEO wants to be updated as necessary until normal operations are restored. If she is not immediately available, then we should work through her admin, S. Spinx.	TG

USING AN ALERT SYSTEM AND INFORMING END USERS

In many instances, malicious code attacks can severely disrupt end user computing functions. There are also cases when end users will be called on to reboot their computers on command, to cease use of their computers for periods of time, and to report new infections that may result from variants of a worm or virus.

A practical mechanism to inform department managers, supervisors, and employees about what is expected and needed from them can greatly aid eradication efforts. The key to successfully communicating with employees at all levels is to keep things simple and easily understandable. Computer incident log

Table 7.5   Log Entries for Alerting Employees

Date/ Time	Log Entry	Staff
May 1 8:20 a.m.	CEO's support staff wrote a memo and hand-distributed it throughout the company notifying users to report incidents, and if they had not yet turned on their computers, they should leave them off until further notice.	TG
8:25 a.m.	A shorter version of the memo was printed in large fonts and posted all over the building, including on all entry doors, by the vending machines, and in the restrooms.	TG
8:55 a.m.	Lists of the computers that the IT staff thought were safe for use was compiled. CEO office staff and the desktop team went to speak to the employees with machines on that list. They were told that they could use their computers, how to identify potential problems, and what they should report to the help desk.	TG

entries from the case study relating to how an alert system is used and how end users were informed about an incident are shown in Table 7.5.

CLEANUP AND RESTORATION

The cleanup and restoration process is often long and tedious, depending on how much automation has been applied to the patching process and antivirus software updates. In some cases, automation can take care of many computers, and the response team may need to do hands-on work on just a few computers. In other situations, the response team may need to spend several days tracking down systems that have been infected to eradicate malicious code.

When computers have not been patched for several months and in many cases for several years, the cleanup and restoration process can require extensive updates to operating systems, browsers, or e-mail programs. Even though most popular antivirus software can be updated through an automated process, many organizations do not take advantage of these capabilities. The basic steps in cleanup and restoration are as follows:

- Identifying computers that are infected

- Removing the malicious code from the computer

- Restoring configurations and systems files that may have been modified by the malicious code

- Installing new patch updates to the operating system, browsers, or other programs

- Updating antivirus software

- Testing the computer to ensure that it boots properly and that the patched applications work properly

- Recovering damaged documents or files that the computer user created and the malicious code damaged or destroyed

Computer incident log entries from the case study relating to cleanup and restoration steps of an incident are shown in Table 7.6.

Table 7.6   Log Entries for Cleanup and Restoration

Date/ Time	Log Entry	Staff
May 1 9:15 a.m.	Desktop team determined that many people on the second floor ignored the warning to not turn on their computers. Many of these machines are infected.	TG
9:20 a.m.	Most computers that are infected have been disconnected from the network.	FR
9:25 a.m.	B. Simons provided the CEO with an update on the status of the infections and the actions of end users.	TG
9:30 a.m.	Desktop team is working on the second floor on eradication and to patch systems and install updated antivirus software. Estimated time per machine is 30 to 45 minutes.	FR

Table 7.6   Log Entries for Cleanup and Restoration (continued)

Date/ Time	Log Entry	Staff
9:35 a.m.	We do not have an accurate map of the network, and there are unidentified infected computers located in various parts of the building.	FR
10:45 a.m.	Some employees in the west wing of the first floor have refused to let the desktop team work on their computers.	TG
10:55 a.m.	B. Simons provided the CEO with an update on the status of the infections and alerted her that some employees will not let the team work on their computers.	TG
11:15 a.m.	The employees that have refused help are now on the low-priority list. It will be a day or so before they are helped.	TG
11:20 a.m.	The search for rogue computers has started. CEO's staff and two members of the desktop team are searching parts of the building.	FR
11:25 a.m.	The first variant of MayDay has been received. It does not pose a threat to the computers we patched and installed updated antivirus software on.	TG

CONTROLLING AND CAPTURING MALICIOUS CODE

Controlling malicious code obviously requires several steps, including patching systems, updating antivirus software, and warning end users of potential. It is also helpful to capture a sampling of viruses or worms that are attempting to infect systems. This sampling allows the computer incident response team to test code to determine if the virus is morphing and to identify new variants that may be attempting to infect systems.

In the case study, the network manager and team leader sampled code throughout the day and identified several new variants. The response team also found previously unknown computers on the network that were a source of infections and had active Trojans that were sending files out of the building.

Table 7.7 Log Entries for Controlling and Capturing Code

Date/ Time	Log Entry	Staff
May 1 11:30 a.m.	Comparisons were made of several samples of the worm, and it was confirmed that the two known variants of MayDay are consistently attempting to infect systems.	TG
12:15 p.m.	Sporadic burst of traffic keeps appearing on the network. Packets were captured and analyzed. Contents included parts of documents and graphic files.	TG
12:30 p.m.	The desktop team has patched and updated antivirus software on 20 more computers on the second floor. Operations have been restored for those users.	FR
1:30 p.m.	A third and fourth variant of MayDay have been hitting the network.	TG
1:40 p.m.	The search team has found several computers in the basement level of the west wing that the IT department did not know about. B. Simons and FR went to examine the systems.	TG
1:50 p.m.	The search team has determined that there are active Trojans on several of the computers in the basement of the west wing. The Trojans were moving proprietary documents out of the building.	TG

Computer incident log entries from the case study relating to controlling and capturing malicious code during an incident response are shown in Table 7.7.

IDENTIFYING THE SOURCE OF MALICIOUS CODE

In most cases, identifying the source of malicious code is pretty basic. When there is a large outbreak of worms or viruses, most organizations are recipients of several copies. Although many organizations have built strong defenses against malicious code attacks, IT security personnel are on alert during outbreaks. Many things need to be monitored during an outbreak, including the emergence of variants of known malicious code as well as new code that may take advantage of recently discovered vulnerabilities.

Another possibility that should be monitored is an attacker that targets a specific system or organization during an outbreak. In the case study, the response team discovered unusual activity on the network and subsequently found systems from which a Trojan was sending files. The Trojan was not a result of the current outbreak but was activated during the attack to move specific files.

In this case, the perpetrator was hoping that he could use the cover of the attack to steal data using a different malicious program other than the ones the defenders were looking for at the time. In this case, the attacker also did not count on there being new staff to defend against the attack. Computer incident log entries from the case study relating to identifying the source of malicious code during an incident are shown in Table 7.8.

Table 7.8   Log Entries for Identifying Source of Malicious Code

Date/ Time	Log Entry	Staff
May 1 1:55 p.m.	Most of the malicious code is the result of the outbreak of MayDay and its variants. There was an additional active Trojan discovered on three computers in the basement of the west wing.	TG
2:00 P.M	The IT manager, B. Simons, informed the computer incident response team that she had similar experiences in the past and she was going to recommend that the CEO call the FBI. All team members have been directed to not discuss the incident with anybody except the IT staff and the CEO's staff. In addition, we are not to use e-mail for anything related to this incident.	FR
2:05 p.m.	The active Trojan is code that is readily available from several sources on the Internet. Specific files were being moved from three computers to an FTP site. We have identified the address of the FTP site.	FR

Table 7.8 Log Entries for Identifying Source of Malicious Code (continued)

Date/ Time	Log Entry	Staff
2:15 p.m.	The desktop team has determined the user ID of the last person to access the computers with the active Trojan. That ID belongs to an employee who has not worked at the company for two years.	RR
2:20 p.m.	The CEO's office is gathering details on the project for the computers where the active code was found.	TG
2:30 p.m.	The CEO's office has requested that details about the users and the project where the active Trojan was found not be entered into the log. It is likely that law enforcement authorities will be called in. Subsequent details about this part of the response will be kept confidential with the CEO.	TG

PRESERVING EVIDENCE

In a situation where an organization is specifically targeted by an attacker, it is important to preserve as much evidence as possible for use by law enforcement authorities. In the case study, the computer incident response team disconnected the network cables that attached three computers that had a Trojan that was moving files out of the building. The response team also started to assemble information about what they did to find the computers and determine what problems had occurred. Computer incident log entries from the case study relating to the preservation of evidence during an incident are shown in Table 7.9.

WHEN TO CALL LAW ENFORCEMENT AND WHAT TO EXPECT

If an incident is reported to law enforcement authorities, it is advisable that the senior manager in the organization make the decision to report. Many organizations are hesitant to call in law enforcement because they do not know what to expect during an investigation. Other organizations are concerned about potential scandals that could be created by an investigation or a court case. In

Table 7.9   Log Entries for Preserving Evidence

Date/ Time	Log Entry	Staff
May 1 2:45 p.m.	The three computers with the active Trojan have been disconnected from the network and were left running.	FR
2:50 p.m.	B. Simons has directed IT staff to minimally disrupt the room where the three computers were found. Papers should not be moved around, and we should note any specific actions we take with computers.	FR
2:55 p.m.	The room where the three computers are located has been equipped with a new lock. The CEO's office and the IT manager have the only keys.	FR
3:10 p.m.	The CEO's office has compiled information on the people who had access to the room with the three infected computers. Background information on the project for which the computers are used was also assembled.	FR
3:45 p.m.	Data to describe the activity of the Trojan is being assembled, along with an explanation of what the response team did to find and disable the computer systems.	TG

addition, many managers believe that the expenses for legal counsel to protect the interests of the organization during a court case are excessive.

What the computer incident response team and organization management should expect from law enforcement and what should be done to aid in the investigation is covered in Chapter 4. Although the case study company, Heartfield Enterprises, did not have procedures in place to deal with such an incident, the IT manager had past experience from which she learned the recommended steps, including the following:

- The CEO responded to the incident quickly and called the FBI on the same day that the problem was discovered.

- The computer incident response team disconnected the computer from the network but did not stop system processes or tamper with files.

- The computer incident response team was directed not to discuss its findings with people outside the IT department or the CEO's office and not to use e-mail in case the perpetrator was capable of monitoring the messages.

- Points of contact where established to assist the investigators.

- Copies were made of files that the Trojan copied or was going to copy.

- Heartfield Enterprises staff did not contact any of the people who could have been responsible for the Trojan.

- Information was organized to help investigators.

Computer incident log entries from the case study relating to calling law enforcement because of an incident are shown in Table 7.10.

ENTERPRISE-WIDE ERADICATION

Eradication of malicious code from all of the computers in an organization can sometimes take several days. This can be a frustrating process, and many response teams leave just a few people active to clean up computers that may have been infected and then powered down because an employee went on vacation or sick leave. Sometimes employees are on leave when an outbreak occurs, and when they come back they are unaware of any problems. If their computers were not patched during the incident, they can end up with a virus. These are all minor but irritating aspects of enterprise-wide eradication, but all of the details need to be addressed.

It is also becoming more common that variants of worms and viruses appear within hours or days of the original event. Some of these variants are designed with a slightly different twist than the original. Malicious code writers can wait to see what the common fix is for the original and then utilize the functionality of the new virus to take advantage of a vulnerability that was not eliminated by the patch or fix for the original malicious code.

Log entries for this phase are basically a continuation of those that began during the cleanup and restoration phase. Estimates of the time it takes per

Table 7.10   Log Entries for Calling Law Enforcement

Date/ Time	Log Entry	Staff
May 1 3:50 p.m.	The FBI has been called about the incident, and all IT staff are to be prepared to answer questions at 9:30 tomorrow morning.	TG
4:10 p.m.	Acting on the advice of the FBI regarding designating a point of contact (POC) for the investigators, B. Simon was designated the POC for IT issues and S. Spinx, the president's assistant, was designated as POC for all other areas.	TG
4:15 p.m.	RR was assigned to make copies of all of the files on the computers with the active Trojans. ZIP disks will be used for storage, and copies will be kept in the IT department and the CEO's office.	TG
4:25 p.m.	LC was assigned the task of working with S. Spinx to determine the exact nature and approximate value of the information in the files moved by the Trojan.	TG
4:30 p.m.	TG and FR were assigned the task of documenting IT-related information for investigators, including the following: -Date, time, and duration of incident. -Physical locations of computer systems compromised -If the systems were ever worked on by a contractor -If the affected systems are critical to any mission -The nature of the attack -Description of the Trojan	TG

computer and the number of staff members working on the cleanup should be noted in the log. This information can be helpful during the lessons learned phase. Computer incident log entries from the case study relating to the eradication of malicious code during an incident are shown in Table 7.11.

Table 7.11 Log Entries for Eradication

Date/ Time	Log Entry	Staff
May 1 5:30 p.m.	A total of 40 computers were cleaned, patched, and equipped with updated antivirus software today. There are about 60 more to be done.	TG
6:00 p.m.	It was determined that only three of the approximately 100 systems that the IT department had patched and updated software for during the last several weeks were infected by MayDay.	FR
6:45 p.m.	After the offices were closed, IT staff removed the network cables from all of the computers they had not worked on yet.	TG
7:00 p.m.	B. Simon briefed the CEO on the status of the cleanup and restoration process.	TG
May 2 7:30 a.m.	The desktop team is working on computers in three departments. The process has been partially automated but still takes about 30 minutes per computer. The team will work until 9:30 a.m., when they need to be back for the initial FBI interview.	TG

RETURNING TO NORMAL OPERATIONS

Once enterprise-wide eradication is achieved and all systems are cleaned and restored to normal operations, there may still be pending issues. This is a good time to ask members of the computer incident response team to start compiling notes for the lessons learned analysis phase. It is also helpful to examine if any additional software licenses are needed or if any particular computer system or network equipment has problems that need to be addressed in the future. Any pending items relating to the investigation of the incident by law enforcement authorities should also be noted. Computer incident log entries from the case study relating to returning to normal operations after an incident are shown in Table 7.12.

Table 7.12 Log Entries for Returning to Normal Operations

Date/ Time	Log Entry	Staff
May 2 9:30 a.m.	Meeting was held with the FBI, and staff was questioned about various aspects of the incident. The response team did a walk-through of the tasks they performed to locate the machines and disconnect them from the network. The FBI took the three infected computers to their forensics lab.	TG
1:30 p.m.	The desktop team has cleaned and restored 20 more machines, and there are about 40 more to be done. One lab will still not let the team in to work on the 20 or so computers they own.	TG
1:45 p.m.	The network is fully operational, but the one lab that will not let the desktop team work on their systems will not be connected until the machines meet standards set by the IT department.	FR
1:50 p.m.	We have decided to evaluate purchasing new gateway equipment and routers and will plan on a network monitoring software upgrade during the next quarter.	FR
2:00 p.m.	The desktop team reports that we need additional licenses for antivirus software, and the order has been placed.	RR
2:05 p.m.	The desktop team has noted that several monitors should be replaced and that about 20 computers are running very old versions of office productivity software that could be upgraded. There are also several printers that need maintenance.	RR
4:00 p.m.	B. Simon has scheduled a lessons learned session for lunchtime tomorrow. All IT staff are expected to provide a brief report and make recommendations.	TG
5:30 p.m.	The desktop team reports that 10 computers on the second floor need to be cleaned, updated, and restored. The lab on the first floor that has refused to let the team work on their computers has agreed to let work be done tomorrow.	RR

ANALYZING LESSONS LEARNED

Analyzing lessons is an important part of the computer incident response process. It is best to have such sessions as the incident is winding down so team members do not forget what they observed or experienced. It is helpful to record the comments from the team and set agenda items for various divisions of the IT department. It is also advisable to hold periodic reviews of the progress that has been made to accomplish those agenda items. Computer incident log entries from the case study relating to the analysis of lessons learned phases of an incident are shown in Table 7.13.

Table 7.13 Log Entries for Analyzing Lessons Learned

Date/ Time	Log Entry	Staff
May 3 1:00 p.m.	Lessons learned session was held with the IT staff, CEO, and the CEO's assistant. Entries are listed for each participant in the session.	TG
	Well, the major thing I learned is that we need to spend more time getting a handle on the network. Since none of us built it, we need good documentation of the wiring scheme and what is hooked to the network and from where. We have been working in that direction, but this bug hit before we were done. We also need to set some policies in place about what the departments can and cannot do with the network, such as building their own wireless LAN.	FR
	I found the employees to be really lacking in training on how to use their computers and especially in how to deal with a malicious code attack. Most of the people I worked with were grateful for the help and seemed to be interested in learning more. I spent a lot of time answering questions after I had their computers up and running. The questions usually started by, "Thank you, and oh, BTW do you know how to blank? Or, Could you help me with a blank blank blank?"	RR

Table 7.13 Log Entries for Analyzing Lessons Learned (continued)

Date/ Time	Log Entry	Staff
	There are still some angry people in some of the labs. I am sure it has to do with Tonya taking over the company and her efforts to implement enterprise-wide systems. They feel like they are losing control, so I think we need to deal with that somehow.	LC
	It is more complicated than just the resistance to a new, young, attractive, and female CEO. There is a lot of discomfort about computers and more so with the older people and especially with the older men. So any approach we take on training needs to take that into consideration.	LK
	We clearly have not had a good handle on the desktop. The computers I worked on really need some work. They had not been patched in years. They also have several different versions of office software, as well as some packages I have not even heard of. The configurations are all over the map, and several monitors are old and fluttery. So I think we need a comprehensive approach on the desktops.	FR
	We need a full set of policies on appropriate use, training, incident response, network rights, and we need all of the managers to endorse and help enforce those policies.	BS
1:45 p.m.	The comments of the computer incident we made into action items and plans were to be developed to achieve all of the objectives. A follow-up meeting to see what has been accomplished on all of the items is scheduled for August 1.	TG
2:00 p.m.	Log closed	TG

ACTION STEPS TO COMBAT MALICIOUS CODE ATTACKS

The material in this chapter illustrates how an organization may respond to a malicious code attack. As steps are taken to defend against malicious code attacks, managers, planners, trainers, and technical staff should understand how IT management procedures can help make computer incident response faster and easier, including the following:

- How a complete inventory of all computers and networking equipment in the organization, including its configuration and patch status, can help support quick action when patches or other interventions are required to stop attacks.

- How having complete documentation on how networks are designed and configured can enable staff to better monitor traffic and identify potential incidents.

- How having departmental information security officers can help coordinate a response and assist in informing end users of problems and attacks.

- What the procedures are to collect information to determine if a crime has been committed and how to notify law enforcement agencies.

- How to structure a lessons learned process to feedback new knowledge into the IT management practices and response procedures of an organization.

Organizations can take several steps to help reduce the impact of malicious code attacks. Recommended steps are included at the end of each chapter. The action steps listed in Table 7.14 are designed to help an organization improve computer incident response procedures.

Table 7.14   Action Steps to Combat Malicious Code Attacks

Number	Action Step
7.1	Evaluate the condition of the computer and networking equipment inventory sheets to determine if the location, configuration, and patch status of all systems is accurately recorded.

Table 7.14 Action Steps to Combat Malicious Code Attacks (continued)

Number	Action Step
7.2	Review the first report, confirmation, and mobilization procedures to determine if they are current in content and adequate in scope to mobilize a response to an attack.
7.3	Review the process to notify management, alert departments, and inform end users to determine if they are current in content and adequate in scope to mobilize a response to an attack.
7.4	Review the cleanup and restoration procedures to determine if they are current in content and adequate in scope to facilitate recovery from an attack.
7.5	Review the procedures for identifying the source of an attack to determine if they are current in content and adequate in scope to facilitate recovery from an attack.
7.6	Review the procedures for preserving evidence of a crime to determine if they are current in content and adequate in scope to meet the needs of reporting a crime to law enforcement agencies.
7.7	Review the procedures for notifying law enforcement that a computer crime has occurred to determine if they are current in content and adequate in scope to meet the needs of the organization.
7.8	Review the procedures for eradication of infections and restoring operations to normal to determine if they are current in content and adequate in scope to meet the needs of the organization.
7.9	Review the processes of analyzing and acting on lessons learned from an incident to determine if they can help the organization improve response.
7.10	Once these reviews have been completed, convene the malicious code attack working group to determine what recommendations should be made to various departments in the organization.

8
Model Training Program for End Users

Training employees to identify malicious code, report attacks, and participate in the response to incidents is one of the most important steps an organization can take when developing defensive measures. Computer users are the first line of defense against malicious code attacks, and when they are properly trained, they can be an asset. However, as experience shows, employees can inadvertently open an e-mail attachment or visit an infected Web site and literally launch an attack that can take days from which to recover. This chapter provides a model training program that covers the following areas:

- Why the training is important

- The appropriate-use policy for computers and networks

- How the help desk and PC support of the organization works

- Basic information about malicious code attacks

- Basic do's and don'ts of computer usage to prevent attacks

- How to identify potential malicious code attacks

- What employees should do if they suspect code is malicious

- What to expect from the IT department during an incident response

Developing training programs does not need to be complicated. The key point to remember is that the tone and the style of the training program should be a good fit for the organization. The individuals who lead the training session need to be personable and able to communicate with people from a wide variety of backgrounds and education levels. They also need to be able to talk to people who may be clerks, middle managers, professional specialists, or upper-level managers.

It is not likely that the smartest geek in your organization will make the best trainer for this subject. However, it does help to have an IT staff person who works in computer security and has responsibility for malicious code countermeasures assist with the training sessions. Several of the modules in this model program need IT department support during the development process. In addition, IT staff can present part of the material or they can help with questions and answers. One of the best ways to deliver a training session is to have that ideal person who can communicate with all sorts of people explain the basic nontechnical material. Then have an IT specialist explain the material that requires a more technical presentation and greater knowledge to answer questions about the material.

Both trainers and trainees have preferred styles, and it is difficult to accommodate all people when designing a training session. The following actions can help training go smoothly and be more enjoyable:

- Take a participatory approach and facilitate interaction during the training sessions.
- Have colorful and entertaining visual aids.
- Serve refreshments.
- Hold sessions in a pleasant environment.
- Hold sessions in well-ventilated areas.
- Provide comfortable seating.
- Have all the materials, handouts, and any forms that employees must sign well organized and easy to distribute during the session.
- Have ink pens available for employees to sign forms. (Let them keep the pens if they want, they cost less than a dollar each.)
- Provide sufficient stretch breaks.

EXPLAINING WHY THE TRAINING IS IMPORTANT

The first step for any type of training is to explain why it is important that employees learn what is being taught. Employees will have a greater appreciation of what they are learning and of the tasks you want them to do if they can be sold on the importance of the new knowledge and skills. This should be a relatively long module in the training program.

It is the responsibility of the training designers and the trainers to develop and deliver the message of importance. This responsibility can be viewed as an evangelistic recruiting mission. There are several good selling points for malicious code attack prevention training:

- There are legal and regulatory requirements that an organization must comply with, such as banking companies and defense contractors. (Specific regulations and laws can be quoted in the training material.)

- The mission statement of the organization can be used as a focal point if it emphasizes service to customers that should be high quality and continuously available. (The mission statement of the organization can be used in the training material.)

- Malicious code attacks have had a very negative impact on the security of several organizations. (Examples from Chapters 1 and 3 of this book can be included in the training material.)

- The potential consequences of malicious code attacks are very serious and can be described in the training as they were in Chapter 1:

  1. Immediate economic impact can include damage to systems that requires human intervention to repair or replace, disruption of business operations, and delays in transactions and cash flow.

  2. Short-term economic impact can include loss of contracts with other organizations in supply chains or the loss of retail sales, negative impact on an organization's reputation, and a hindrance to developing new business.

  3. Long-term economic impact can include a decline in market valuation and stock price, erosion of investor confidence, and reduced goodwill value.

- In action steps 3.2 and 3.3 (see Chapter 3), the malicious code working group was to collect information about if and how the major attack events reviewed in Chapter 3 affectedyour organization. This material can be used to illustrate the negative consequences of past events.

Table 8.1 Impact of Malicious Code Attack on an Organization

Direct damage to target organization's computer systems
Cost to repair damage or restore target organization's systems and functionality
Decrease in productivity of employees in target organization
Delays in order processing or customer service in target organization
Decrease in productivity in customer's organization because of delays in target organization
Delays in customer's business because of delays in target organization
Negative impact on local economies where target organization is located
Negative impact on local economies where target organization's customers are located
Negative impact on value for individual investors in target organization
Negative impact on value of investment funds holding target organization securities
Negative impact on regional economies where target organization, customer, or investor organizations are located
Negative impact on national economies where target organization, customer, or investor organizations are located

Source: *Implementing Homeland Security in Enterprise IT*, Michael Erbschloe (Digital Press, 2003)

Several visual aids can be used during this part of the training session. In Chapter 1, the discussion of the impact of malicious code attacks included the material in Table 8.1. Any or all of the types of impact can be included as bulleted items in training material for your organization. The methods of measurement are widely recognized and used by organizations all over the world.

Many organizations are now participating in a variety of social responsibility movements. This can be used as a motivating factor for malicious code attack prevention training. If your organization has a strong emphasis on social responsibility, then the material found in *Socially Responsible IT Management* could be helpful in the training session. The book explains 10 principles of social responsibility and how they can help eliminate many of the IT-related

Table 8.2   Principles of Socially Responsible IT Management

Number	Principle
1	Staff IT departments appropriately.
2	Compensate IT workers fairly.
3	Train computer users adequately.
4	Provide ergonomic user environments.
5	Maintain secure and virus-free computer systems.
6	Safeguard the privacy of information.
7	Manage intellectual property ethically.
8	Utilize energy-efficient technology.
9	Recycle used computer equipment properly.
10	Support efforts to reduce the digital divide.

Source: *Socially Responsible IT Management*, Michael Erbschloe (Digital Press, 2002)

problems that organizations now face. Several of the principles directly affect an organization's ability to deal with IT security problems. That concept was explained in Chapter 1. The 10 principles are shown again in Table 8.2. The basic proposition is that organizations should be good cybercitizens and keep their computers secure and free from viruses so they are not responsible for spreading viruses and worms.

The U.S. Federal Trade Commission (FTC) has material on its Web site that you may find helpful to include in your training sessions. The material includes a postcard that can serve as an entertaining graphic in a presentation (see www.ftc.gov/bcp/conline/pubs/postcards/PCD13-infosec.pdf). The FTC Web site also lists other places on the World Wide Web where you may find helpful motivational material, including the following organizations:

- The **National Cyber Security Alliance** (www.staysafeonline.info) is a cooperative effort between industry and government organizations to foster awareness of cybersecurity through educational outreach and public awareness.

- The **GetNetWise.org security section** (security.getnetwise.org) was established to deliver information and materials to consumers to protect their information and networks from theft, misuse, and destruction. The site includes tutorials on how to use common software programs to enhance security and privacy.

- The **National Cyber Alert System** (us-cert.gov) is a partnership between the Department of Homeland Security's National Cyber Security Division (NCSD) and the private sector, which offers the National Cyber Alert System to provide timely information about current and emerging threats to computers and networks.

- The **Cybercitizen Awareness Program** (cybercitizenship.org) educates children and young adults on the dangers and consequences of cybercrime. By reaching out to parents and teachers, the program is designed to establish a broad sense of responsibility and community in an effort to develop in young people smart, ethical, and socially conscious online behavior.

- **BBBOnLine** (www.bbbonline.org) is the arm of the Council of Better Business Bureaus (BBBs) that specifically deals with Web sites. Working in concert with the 142 local BBBs in the United States and Canada, BBBOnLine encourages sound and ethical online business practices through its Privacy program, Reliability program, BBB Code of Online Business Practices, and an international initiative to promote safe e-commerce.

- The **GetNetWise coalition** (www.getnetwise.org) wants Internet users to be only "one click away" from the resources they need to make informed decisions about their family's use of the Internet.

- **Organization for Economic Co-Operation and Development (OECD)** (www.oecd.org/ict/guidelines) member governments have drawn up new *Guidelines for the Security of Information Systems and Networks* in order to counter cyberterrorism, computer viruses, hacking, and other threats.

- The **Computer Crime and Intellectual Property Section (CCIPS)** (www.usdoj.gov/criminal/cybercrime/index.html) attorney staff focuses exclusively on the issues raised by computer and intellectual property crime. Section attorneys advise federal prosecutors and law enforcement agents; comment on and propose legislation; coordinate international efforts to combat computer crime; litigate cases; and train all law enforcement groups.

- **U.S. Department of Education Internet Safety Page** (www.ed.gov/about/offices/list/os/technology/safety.html) is a source for the education community working on goals for educational technology.

- **CyberSmart!** (www.cybersmart.org) provides a comprehensive set of free lesson plans, student activities, and related materials for teachers and families to introduce the skills associated with 21st-century literacy, citizenship, and ethics. These skills provide the building blocks in order for children to be safe, responsible, and effective 21st-century citizens and learners.

- The **CERT Coordination Center (CERT/CC)** (www.cert.org/tech_tips/home_networks.html) is a center of Internet security expertise, located at the Software Engineering Institute, a federally funded research and development center operated by Carnegie Mellon University in Pittsburgh. CERT's information ranges from protecting your system against potential problems to reacting to current problems to predicting future problems.

- **National Institute of Standards and Technology Computer Security Resource Center's Small Business Corner** (csrc.nist.gov/SBC) provides support to improve information systems security. This site focuses on resources for small businesses.

- The **Information Technology Association of America (ITAA)** (www.itaa.org/infosec) seeks to improve the information security of the nation's critical information infrastructure in both the private and public sectors. This site includes links to news articles, press releases, and reports.

- The **Internet Security Alliance** (www.isalliance.org) is a collaborative effort between Carnegie Mellon's CERT/CC and the Electronic Industries Alliance to promote sound information security practices, policies, and technologies that enhance the security of the Internet and global information systems. The ISA recently released a guide to 10 of the highest priority and most frequently recommended security practices for business.

- **Consumer Reports' Cyberspace Invaders site** (www.consumerreports.org/static/0206com0.html) includes practical advice for consumers and a link to *Consumer Reports'* online subscriber security survey. It also includes consumer security product ratings.

- The **Center for Internet Security (CIS)** (www.cisecurity.org) provides methods and tools to improve, measure, monitor, and compare the security status of Internet-connected systems and appliances.

- The **World Bank** (www.worldbank.org) is working to educate policy makers, businesses, consumers of financial services, and others involved in e-finance and e-commerce through an e-security site focusing on the complex tradeoffs and actions needed to manage the risks of fraud and of compromising the security of digital assets. The site serves as a clearinghouse for knowledge on managing the risks associated with open network architectures.

- The **Business Roundtable's Digital Economy Task Force** (www.brtable.org/document.cfm/814) has produced a resource to help CEOs and their senior executives develop a robust, effective program to protect their businesses as they incorporate sophisticated information systems into their operations. The resource includes recommendations for furthering corporate cybersecurity programs; a depiction of the need for not just technology but also policy issues in a successful program; and a list of key government contacts and Internet sites with more information on cybersecurity.

- The **Business Software Alliance (BSA)** (www.bsa.org/usa/policy/security/issue/index.phtml), with programs in 65 countries worldwide, is dedicated to promoting a safe and legal digital world. BSA is the voice of the world's commercial software industry before governments and in the international marketplace. BSA also educates consumers on software management and copyright protection, cybersecurity, trade, e-commerce, and other Internet-related issues.

- The **United States Postal Service** (www.usps.com/privacyoffice/welcome.htm) offers a Web site with information about its comprehensive privacy framework. The site also provides links to other resources and tools dealing with a host of privacy issues.

Once the training material for this module has been assembled and put into your desired format of PowerPoint slides or handouts, the presentation should be rehearsed and tested. This can be done with employees or friends and associates of the training developers and trainers. The key aspect to test this module for is its selling power. The evaluators should be asked to answer the following questions:

1. Does the material convince you that learning how to prevent malicious code attacks is important?

2. Does the material convince you that our organization takes malicious code attack prevention seriously?

3. Does the material motivate you to participate in the training?

4. Does the material inspire you to help the organization prevent malicious code attacks?

5. Did you understand all of the material? (If no, then seek clarification on what was not understandable.)

6. What part of the presentation did you like the most?

7. Which slide or graphic did you like the most?

8. What part of the presentation did you like the least?

9. Which slide or graphic did you like the least?

10. Should anything be added to the presentation?

11. Should anything be taken out of the presentation?

EXPLAINING THE APPROPRIATE-USE POLICY FOR COMPUTERS AND NETWORKS

An appropriate-use policy for computers and networks informs employees what they can and cannot do with an organization's technology assets. Many attorneys recommend that organizations clearly communicate the appropriate-use policies to employees both in writing and in a formal training program. Employees should be trained on the policies and be required to sign a statement that they have received the training and will adhere to the employer's policies on acceptable use of computer systems and networks. This should be a relatively short module in the training program.

If your organization has an appropriate-use policy in place, this training session is a good time to reiterate what the policies are and explain why the policies exist. When appropriate use is explained within the context of computer security and malicious code countermeasures, employees may find the policies more acceptable. When explaining appropriate-use policies, it is a good idea to develop your own do's and don'ts list and use that list as a training aid during this session. Appropriate-use policies are covered in Chapter 6.

This is also an opportunity to explain how appropriate-use policies are enforced. If your organization utilizes any of the methods to control employee computer behaviors that are explained in Chapter 6, those methods can be explained, along with details on how they contribute to malicious code attack prevention. Each method can be illustrated by using examples of problems that have occurred, including the cases in Chapter 3 or any similar incidents that have occurred in your organization. The methods of control discussed in Chapter 6 are as follows:

- Web site blockers and Internet filters
- Cookie spyware blockers
- Pop-up blockers
- Controlling downloads
- SPAM control

Once the training material for this module has been assembled and put into your desired format of PowerPoint slides or handouts, the presentation should be rehearsed and tested. As with other modules, this can be done with employees or friends and associates of the training developers and trainers. It is advisable that legal counsel be involved in crafting the explanation of appropriate-use policies and in the review of this module before it is presented to employees. The key aspect to test this module for is how well it explains and supports the appropriate-use policies and the methods that are used to enforce the policies. The evaluators should be asked to answer the following questions:

1. How well does the material explain appropriate-use policies?
2. Does the material convince you that the appropriate-use policies are justifiable and serve a security-related purpose?

3. Did you understand all of the material? (If no, then seek clarification on what was not understandable.)

4. Does the material inspire you to help the organization prevent malicious code attacks?

5. Does the material motivate you to adhere to appropriate-use policies?

6. What part of the presentation did you like the most?

7. Which slide or graphic did you like the most?

8. What part of the presentation did you like the least?

9. Which slide or graphic did you like the least?

10. Should anything be added to the presentation?

11. Should anything be taken out of the presentation?

EXPLAINING HOW THE HELP DESK AND PC SUPPORT OF THE ORGANIZATION WORKS

It is helpful for employees to know how to get help on computer problems when they need it. It is better that employees contact the IT department or help desk to solve a problem than it is for them to try to solve a computer problem on their own and do damage in the process. This should be a relatively short module in the training program.

Explaining the help desk support function and its role in the everyday operations of the organization and its role in computer incident response helps put IT functions and responsibilities into context for the employees being trained. The goal of this module is to educate as well as to create that warm, fuzzy feeling that the organization wants to help computer users solve problems.

Remember that this session is designed to motivate employees to help counter malicious code attacks. They are asked to do that in several ways, including reporting potential problems, understanding how the alert system functions, and understanding their role in the cleanup and restoration process. Material to present in this module includes the following:

• What the help desk can do for them

• Examples of the types of problems the help desk has solved in the past

• The help desk phone number or e-mail address

- The operational hours of the help desk or help line
- The names of the people who work on the help desk
- The procedures for asking for help or reporting general problems
- If an intranet is in use in your organization that provides computer help pages, the process for accessing those pages should be explained, along with what the pages offer and how to use them.

Once the training material for this module has been assembled and put into your desired format of PowerPoint slides or handouts, the presentation should be rehearsed and tested. The test audience can be similar to those used for other modules. However, it may be more beneficial to use actual employees in testing this module because it is so organization specific. You need to determine if it makes sense to people who will take the steps recommended in the module. The key aspect to test this module for is how well it explains how the help desk actually functions and the type of support it provides. The evaluators should be asked to answer the following questions:

1. How well does the material explain help desk functions?
2. Does the material adequately explain how to contact the help desk?
3. Did you understand all of the material? (If no, then seek clarification on what was not understandable.)
4. Does the material inspire you to work with the help desk?
5. What part of the presentation did you like the most?
6. Which slide or graphic did you like the most?
7. What part of the presentation did you like the least?
8. Which slide or graphic did you like the least?
9. Should anything be added to the presentation?
10. Should anything be taken out of the presentation?

PROVIDING BASIC INFORMATION ABOUT MALICIOUS CODE

It is helpful to explain to employees what malicious code is, what it can do, and how it works. This can be achieved by using the material in Chapter 2. It is important to make the explanations easy to understand, because these modules are designed to train a nontechnical group of people. This should be a relatively long module in the training program. The graphics in Chapter 2 can be used as training aids in this module. Important points to cover about malicious code include the following:

- In general, *malicious code* is any software that impedes the normal operation of a computer or networking device. This software most often executes without the user's consent.

- Malicious code comes in a wide variety of forms and is distributed through an ever-growing number of delivery mechanisms, including the following:

    1. E-mail and other types of viruses
    2. Trojans and other backdoors
    3. Worms
    4. Blended threats
    5. Time bombs
    6. Spyware
    7. Adware
    8. Stealware

- In general, computer viruses replicate and spread from one system to another. Many viruses merely replicate and clog e-mail systems. Some computer viruses have what is called a malicious payload, which is code that can execute commands on computers such as deleting or corrupting files or disabling computer security software.

- The wooden horse that the Greeks reputedly used during the siege of Troy has been conceptually applied to malicious code that allows its creator to execute an unauthorized command or set of commands on a computer infected by the code.

- *Trojan horses* are both problematic and a basic type of malicious code designed primarily to give a hacker access to system files. This gives hackers the ability to change file settings, steal files or passwords, damage files, or monitor user activities on other computers on a network.

- A *worm* is a malicious program that originates on a single computer and searches for other computers connected through a local area network (LAN) or Internet connection. When a worm finds another computer, it will replicate onto that computer and continue to look for other connected computers on which to replicate. A worm will continue to attempt to replicate itself indefinitely or until a self-timing mechanism halts the process.

- Malicious code that is referred to as a *blended threat* is code that can replicate itself in more than one manner, can have more than one type of trigger, and can have multiple task capabilities. A blended threat is often able to move around the Internet, using e-mail virus capabilities as well as worm capabilities. A blended threat attack can also plant a Trojan on a computer.

- One of the very first forms of malicious code was a *time bomb* (or logic bomb), which, when installed, is a dormant code that can be triggered at a future date by a specific event or circumstance. Triggers can be a specific date and time or even a cumulative number of system starts.

- The term *spyware* is used to describe any computer technology that gathers information about a person or organization without their knowledge or consent. Spyware can be installed on a computer through several covert means, including as part of a software virus or as the result of adding a new program.

- Several advertising networks have been accused of using a form of malicious code called *Web bugs* to collect information about computer users to assist in the compilation of personal profiles. These bugs can collect information about the Web sites that an Internet user visits and what he or she does at those Web sites. The information can be stored in databases and used to select what types of banners or advertisements a user is shown.

- *Stealware* is another name often associated with Web bugs or spyware. It is often used by Web sites that have various types of affiliate marketing programs or that are members of affiliate marketing plans. Some peer-to-peer software applications are reported to have stealware attributes

- Note that the terms spyware, stealware, and adware are sometimes used to describe the same or similar types of malicious code.

Because many people have now become more familiar with computer viruses, it can be useful to provide examples of actual malicious code attacks. Chapter 3 provides a historic perspective from which actual cases can be extracted for use in training. It is important to not include too much detail. Examples of what can be presented in this module are as follows:

- Malicious code attacks are constant, and they are increasing in number and in severity. Attackers use various types of malicious code during the attack process.

- In 1999, David Smith of New Jersey wrote the Melissa virus that replicated through e-mail and infected Microsoft Word documents. Melissa would replicate by sending itself to the first 50 addressees in the e-mail program of the recipient's computer. In a three-day period, Melissa infected more than 100,000 computers. Some organizations reported receiving tens of thousands of Melissa e-mail messages in less than an hour.

- May 4, 2000, was one of the most dramatic days in malicious code history. It was the first day on which a virus outbreak received massive and daily coverage in the mass media. Lloyd's of London estimated that the virus cost more than $15 billion in damages. The I Love You code was unique for its time because it was both a virus and worm.

- On July 19, 2001, the Code Red virus infected more than 20,000 systems within 10 minutes and more than 250,000 systems in just under 9 hours. An estimated 975,000 infections occurred worldwide before Code Red subsided. Code Red and Code Red II disrupted both government and business operations, principally by slowing Internet service and forcing some organizations to disconnect from the Internet.

- Many computer security experts called 2003 the Year of the Worm because for 12 months worms spread across the Internet with the intensity of an apocalyptic event. It began in January, when the Slammer worm infected nearly 75,000 servers in 10 minutes. It was widely reported that Slammer clogged Bank of America's ATM network and caused sporadic flight delays for airlines.

- In August, the worm Blaster, Welchia worm, Sobig, and their variants hit the Internet with severe force, spreading via e-mail and stealing addresses from infected computers. It replicated so fast that at one point, one out of every seventeen e-mail messages traveling through the Internet was a copy of Sobig. In China, the August onslaught may have affected 85 percent of Internet-connected computers. Sobig variants plagued the Internet for the remainder of 2003, replicating more than 1 million copies per month.

- In January 2004, just as the Department of Homeland Security (DHS) launched its new centralized system to alert the country to threats to computer systems, a worm called MyDoom was wreaking havoc on thousands of Internet users. MyDoom disguised itself as e-mail that was not delivered properly as an attempt to get recipients to open attachments that launch the malicious code. Some organizations reported they were blocking more than 100,000 MyDoom-infected e-mails per hour. At another point, more than 40 percent of Internet traffic consisted of MyDoom-infected e-mail messages. During its spread, MyDoom created hundreds of millions of e-mail messages.

These examples can be combined with material that was created by the training subcommittee of the malicious code work group recommended in action steps 3.2, 3.3, and 3.4 (see Chapter 3). This includes information on how the major malicious code events reviewed in Chapter 3 have affected your organization and how your organization responded to those events.

Once the training material for this module has been assembled and put into your desired format of PowerPoint slides or handouts, the presentation should be rehearsed and tested. The test audience can be similar to those used for other modules. However, the material should be reviewed by a member of the IT staff who works on malicious code defenses to ensure that it is accurate. If this module can be presented by an IT staff person, it can include more details or more technical content if you desire. The key aspect to test this module for is how well it explains how malicious code attacks work. The evaluators should be asked to answer the following questions:

1. How well does the presentation explain malicious code attacks?

2. Did you understand all of the material? (If no, then seek clarification on what was not understandable.)

3. Does the material inspire you to work to help the organization defend against malicious code attacks?

4. Was the material too technical?

5. What part of the presentation did you like the most?

6. Which slide or graphic did you like the most?

7. What part of the presentation did you like the least?

8. Which slide or graphic did you like the least?

9. Should anything be added to the presentation?

10. Should anything be taken out of the presentation?

COVERING THE BASIC DO'S AND DON'TS OF COMPUTER USAGE TO PREVENT ATTACKS

After the basics of malicious code attacks are covered, it is a good opportunity reinforce some do's and don'ts of Internet use that can prevent attacks from occurring. This should be a relatively short module in the training program. The material will probably not require more than two PowerPoint slides. However, interactive discussion and a question-and-answer format can greatly help reinforce good computing and Internet usage habits.

During modules covering do's and don'ts, participants often ask lengthy questions or try to show off their computer knowledge. If an IT staff person is presenting this module, this type of discussion is usually not problematic. If a nontechnical person is making this presentation, he or she should be cautious about getting into details that he or she may not fully understand.

The material for this module should be created by the IT staff who are responsible for security and malicious code defenses. Some of the more important do's and don'ts to convey to employees include the following:

Things not to do:

• Disable or interfere with the antivirus software on your computer.

• Open e-mail from unknown sources.

- Open e-mail attachments unless you know whom they are from.

- Share access to your computers with strangers.

- Let somebody else use your user ID and password.

- Interfere with the installation of software patches.

- Let Web sites you visit install code on your computer.

Things to do:

- Scan e-mail attachments with antivirus software before opening them. When in doubt, delete suspicious e-mail.

- Scan files on floppy disks before you open them.

- Use hard-to-guess passwords.

- Change your passwords often.

- Back up your computer data and files.

- Be cautious when downloading files from the Internet.

Once the training material for this module has been assembled and put into your desired format of PowerPoint slides or handouts, the presentation should be rehearsed and tested. The test audience can be similar to those used for other modules. If this module can be presented by an IT staff person, it can include more details or more technical content if you desire. The key aspect to test this module for is if the training session participants understand how to implement the do's and don'ts. The evaluators should be asked to answer the following questions:

1. How well does the presentation explain the do's and don'ts of Internet use?

2. Can you act on the advice that is provided in the presentation?

3. Did you understand all of the material? (If no, then seek clarification on what was not understandable.)

4. Does the material inspire you to work to help the organization defend against malicious code attacks?

5. Should anything be added to the presentation?

6. Should anything be taken out of the presentation?

EXPLAINING HOW TO IDENTIFY AND REPORT MALICIOUS CODE

Employees will be able to contribute more to the malicious code attack prevention efforts if they know what kind of events or incidents to report to the IT department. The material for this module should be developed by the IT staff person responsible for malicious code countermeasures. It is advisable to keep this material basic, and only one or two PowerPoint slides are needed. This should be a relatively short module in the training program.

The best way to communicate what employees should be watching for and report to the IT department is by describing the type of computer behaviors and problems that may indicate that their computer has been infected. This includes the following:

- Unusual activity in the e-mail program
- Missing or corrupted files
- Programs that fail to execute when opened
- Keyboard locking up frequently
- Computer often reboots on its own

The explanation of how to report problems that can be caused by malicious code to the IT department should be straightforward. There should be a brief explanation, along with the telephone number or e-mail address they should use to file the report. The basic steps to establish a reporting system are covered in Chapter 5.

Once the training material for this module has been assembled and put into your desired format of PowerPoint slides or handouts, the presentation should be rehearsed and tested. The test audience can be similar to those used for other modules. If this module can be presented by an IT staff person, it will be easier to deal with questions and answers. The key aspect to test this module for is how well it explains what computer behaviors users should be concerned about and how they should report these incidents to the IT department. The evaluators should be asked to answer the following questions:

1. How well does the presentation explain the behaviors that may indicate if a malicious code attack has occurred?

2. How well does the presentation explain how employees should report suspected malicious code attacks?

3. Did you understand all of the material? (If no, then seek clarification on what was not understandable.)

4. Does the material inspire you to work to help the organization defend against malicious code attacks?

5. Was the material too technical?

EXPLAINING WHAT EMPLOYEES SHOULD EXPECT FROM THE IT DEPARTMENT DURING INCIDENT RESPONSE

Employees will feel more involved in the efforts to combat malicious code attacks if they are made aware of what the computer incident response process is and how it works. This module does not have to go into great detail, but it should explain the process from beginning to end. An IT staff person who works on the computer incident response team should develop the content for this module, and the material should be organization specific. The steps in the response process are covered in Chapter 7 and include how the IT department does the following:

- Receives the first reports about the malicious code attack
- Confirms that an attack is in progress
- Mobilizes the computer incident response team
- Notifies management that there is a problem
- Uses the alert system to inform department managers
- How and when end users will be informed about the attack
- What employees should do to help with incident response
- How the cleanup and restoration process works
- How malicious code is controlled
- How the IT department works to identify the source of the malicious code
- How attack responses are analyzed to determine the lessons learned

Each of these areas can be covered with one or two PowerPoint slides. If a staff person from the IT department is presenting this module, the printed material can be complemented with anecdotal information. People do tend to like to tell and hear war stories.

The key thing to bear in mind about this module is when employees are being trained on what is expected of them and how they can help during incident response, the information needs to be presented in a straightforward and easy-to-understand manner. Because the information in this module is organization specific, it is important to make sure that the information reflects the reality of what happens during a computer incident response.

Once the training material for this module has been assembled and put into your desired format of PowerPoint slides or handouts, the presentation should be rehearsed and tested. The test audience for this module should include employees who are familiar with the computer incident response process as well as people who are not familiar with the process. This mix of test audiences allows training developers to test the accuracy and clarity of the material and if the presentation is understandable by those who are not familiar with the process. The key aspect to test this module for is how well it explains how the computer incident response process works. The evaluators should be asked to answer the following questions:

1. How well does the presentation explain each step in the computer incident response process?

2. Did you understand all of the material? (If no, then seek clarification on what was not understandable.)

3. Does the material inspire you to work to help the organization defend against malicious code attacks?

4. Was the material too technical?

5. What part of the presentation did you like the most?

6. Which slide or graphic did you like the most?

7. What part of the presentation did you like the least?

8. Which slide or graphic did you like the least?

9. Should anything be added to the presentation?

10. Should anything be taken out of the presentation?

PERFORMING THE ADMINISTRATIVE ASPECTS OF A TRAINING PROGRAM

A specialized training department often handles the administrative aspects of training programs in large organizations. In some organizations, the training function is a subpart of the Human Resources department. Regardless of how your organization is structured, several administrative aspects of a training program must be managed, including the following:

- Scheduling training sessions
- Recruiting and training trainers
- Identifying which employees need training
- Enrolling employees in training sessions
- Maintaining records of the employees who have attended training
- Scheduling employees for appropriate refresher courses
- Arranging for a training facility
- Reproducing and distributing training materials
- Analyzing the results of course evaluations done by participants

In most organizations, one person could perform most of these functions on a part-time basis. In larger and geographically dispersed organizations, it may take several people to perform the various functions. If there is a training department in your organization, it is advisable to work with them to manage or find people to manage the necessary training functions. If there is not a training department to work with, then a coordinator from the Human Resources department or the IT department could handle much of the work that needs to be done.

ACTION STEPS TO COMBAT MALICIOUS CODE ATTACKS

The material in this chapter shows how to develop a malicious code attack prevention training program for end users. It builds on the material presented in other chapters and provides pointers on how to best use the material in those chapters to achieve the training goals. Training developers and trainers should keep several points in mind when designing and implementing a training program:

- The training process and material should be motivational and sell the concepts and processes to employees as opposed to being dictatorial and imposing the process.
- To help the selling process, it is important to make the training entertaining and enjoyable.
- Each module should be tested with different audiences.
- The training material should be kept up to date.
- The PowerPoint slides should not be cluttered, and participants sitting in the back of the room should be able to easily read the slides.
- Participants should be asked to complete a brief evaluation form after attending the training. (Keep it brief and do not attempt to extract too much detail about specific slides or modules.)

The action steps listed in Table 8.3 are designed to help an organization develop and launch a training program to help reduce the impact of malicious code attacks.

Table 8.3   Action Steps to Develop Training for Malicious Code Attack Prevention

Number	Action Step
8.1	Designate a coordinator to lead the development of the malicious code prevention training program.
8.2	Designate an IT staff person to be the primary point of contact for the training coordinator.
8.3	Establish a project schedule for the development and testing of the training material.
8.4	Designate an HR staff person to coordinate the record-keeping process for employees who have participated in the training.
8.5	Initiate the training process.

Table 8.3 Action Steps to Develop Training for Malicious Code Attack Prevention (continued)

Number	Action Step
8.6	After several training sessions have taken place, evaluate the response to the training, and determine if any changes should be made to the material or the process.

9
The Future of Malicious Code

There are opposing perspectives on the future of malicious code attacks. The optimists contend that a range of off-the-shelf computer software as well as specialty security products will improve sufficiently to counter the type of attacks that now occur. The pessimists contend that malicious code writers will continue to get more sophisticated and will be able to outpace the improvements in software.

There are also those who believe that cyberwarfare is the future of conflict. The concept of a digital Pearl Harbor has been under discussion for more than a decade. There are two sides to this argument as well. The optimists contend that large-scale cyberattacks are so difficult that very few nations could actually mount such offensive maneuvers, and most of those nations are allies of the United States. The pessimists point to the biting success that young hackers have had penetrating NASA and Department of Defense (DoD) computers as well as many critical emergency service systems and contend that if amateurs can do it, then so can organized terrorists.

From a business perspective, it is foolish to think that the problem of malicious code attacks will be either self-solving or self-dissolving. The security-conscious manager has little choice but to work on today's defenses as well as carefully consider how computers and networks are deployed in the future. The consequences for lax security are continuously growing. New legal requirements for information security are touching almost every organization. This chapter examines several aspects of the future of malicious code attacks that security planners should be aware of, including the following:

•   Military-style information warfare

•   Open-source information warfare

- Militancy and social action

- Homeland security efforts.

MILITARY-STYLE INFORMATION WARFARE

The historical military perspective on information warfare focused on the protection or destruction of military weapons systems or communications infrastructure. During the 1990s, the military view of information warfare rapidly evolved. Much of this evolution was driven by the widespread availability of the Internet and the corresponding growth in the number of people who could become attackers and the number of things that could be attacked.

The terrorist attacks of 2001 also changed the view of the military toward information warfare, at least in the United States. The Northern Command, that group of military units that is responsible for protecting the United States homeland, now faces a potential threat of more attacks on American soil or perhaps even in American cyberspace.

There is a need for extraordinary action to deal with the present and emerging challenges of defending against possible information warfare attacks on facilities, information, computer systems, and networks of the United States, according to a task force of the Defense Science Board.[1] Such attacks would seriously affect the ability of the DoD to carry out its assigned missions and functions. The task force observed an increasing dependency on the Defense Information Infrastructure and increasing doctrinal assumptions regarding the continued availability of that infrastructure. The task force concluded that this dependency and these assumptions are ingredients in a recipe for a national security disaster.

The report was the third consecutive effort of the Board that had made similar recommendations to better prepare the DoD for the challenges of information warfare. Accordingly, the Board recommend a series of more than 50 actions designed to better prepare the DoD for this new form of warfare, beginning with identification of an accountable focal point within the DoD for all information warfare activities. The task force established to conduct the studies were asked to do the following:

- Identify the information users of national interest who can be attacked through the shared elements of the national information infrastructure.

- Determine the scope of national information interests to be defended by information warfare defense and deterrence capabilities.

- Characterize the procedures, processes, and mechanisms required to defend against various classes of threats to the national information infrastructure and the information users of national interest.

- Identify the indications and warning, tactical warning, and attack assessment procedures, processes, and mechanisms needed to anticipate, detect, and characterize attacks on the national information infrastructure and/or attacks on the information users of national interest.

- Identify the reasonable roles of government and the private sector, alone and in concert, in creating, managing, and operating a national information warfare–defense capability.

- Provide specific guidelines for implementation of the Task Force's recommendations.

The task force asserted that, in general, cyberinfrastructures are extremely reliable and available because they have been designed to respond to disruptions, particularly those caused by natural phenomena. Redundancy and diverse routing are two examples of design techniques used to improve reliability and availability. However, deregulation and increased competition cause companies operating these infrastructures to rely more heavily on information technology to centralize control of their operations, to support critical functions, and to deliver goods and services. Centralization and reliance on broadly networked information systems increase the vulnerabilities of the infrastructures and the likelihood of disruptions or malevolent attacks.

The information users of national interest who can be attacked through the shared elements of the national information infrastructure are those responsible for performing the critical functions necessary for the delivery of the goods and services on which our political, military, and economic interests depend.

A critical observation that was made is that offensive information warfare is attractive to many because it is cheap in relation to the cost of developing, maintaining, and using advanced military capabilities. It may cost little to suborn an insider, create false information, manipulate information, or launch malicious logic-based weapons against an information system connected to the globally shared telecommunications infrastructure. The latter option is particularly attractive; the latest information on how to exploit many of the design attributes and security flaws of commercial computer software is freely available on the Internet.

In addition, attackers may be attracted to information warfare by the potential for large, nonlinear outputs from modest inputs. This is possible because the information and information systems subject to offensive information warfare attack may only be a minor cost component of a function or activity of interest: the database of the items in a warehouse costs much less than the physical items stored in the warehouse.

The task force stipulated that the DoD must preserve its ability to fulfill its basic missions. To do that, the DoD must be concerned about the ensured operation of the critical functions and the availability of information necessary to fulfill those missions. The intertwined nature of the functions of national interest and supporting infrastructures add to the complexity: there are critical functions that have national security implications and that must be defended, and there are critical portions of the infrastructures that are necessary for the operation of DoD and national functions. The concept for defending the information infrastructure and the information components of other critical infrastructures includes the following principles:

- Critical functions must be capable of being performed in the presence of information warfare attacks.

- Some minimum essential infrastructure capability must exist to support these critical functions.

- Point and layered defenses are preferable to area defenses.

- The infrastructure must be designed to function in the presence of failed components, systems, and networks. The risk associated with failed components, systems, and networks must be managed because it cannot be avoided.

- The infrastructure control functions should not depend on normal operation of the infrastructure.

- The infrastructure must be capable of being repaired.

For the third year in a row, the Task Force made key recommendations it considered to be imperative:

1. Designate an accountable information warfare focal point.
2. Organize for information warfare defense.
3. Increase awareness about information warfare needs.
4. Assess infrastructure dependencies and vulnerabilities.
5. Define threat conditions and responses.
6. Assess information warfare defense readiness.
7. "Raise the bar" (with high-payoff, low-cost items) for information warfare.
8. Establish a minimum essential information infrastructure.
9. Focus the R&D for information warfare.
10. Staff for success in information warfare.
11. Resolve the legal issues about information warfare.
12. Participate fully in critical infrastructure protection.
13. Provide the resources for information warfare.

When examining the potential for information warfare activities, the task force concluded that the potential for a criminal or nongovernmental attack for economic purposes must be considered. Information is the basis for the global economy. Money is information; only approximately 10 percent of the time does it exist in physical form. As information systems are increasingly used for financial transactions at all levels, it is natural to expect all levels of criminals to target information systems in order to achieve some gain.

The increasing interconnectivity of information systems makes them a tempting target for political dissidents. Activities of interest to this group include spreading the basic message of their cause by a variety of means as well as inviting others to actions. An example is the political dissident in this country who sent out e-mails urging folks to send e-mail bombs to the White House server.

By attacking those targets in a highly visible way, the terrorist hopes to cause the media to provide a great deal of publicity of the action, thereby further disseminating the message of fear and uncertainty. Threats included the following:

- *The incompetent threat* is an amateur who by some means (perhaps by following a hacker recipe or by accident) manages to perform some action that exploits or exacerbates a vulnerability. This category could include a poorly trained systems administrator who assigns privilege groups incorrectly, which would then allow a more nefarious threat to claim more privileges on a system than would be warranted.

- *The hacker threat* implies a person with more technical knowledge who understands to some degree the processes used and has the intent to violate the security or defenses of a target to one degree or another. The hacker threat is broad in motivation, ranging from those who are mostly just curious to those who commit acts of vandalism.

- *The disgruntled employee threat* is the ultimate insider threat: the individual who is inside the organization and trusted. This threat is the most difficult to detect because insiders have legitimate access.

- A significant threat that cannot be discounted includes activities engaged on behalf of competitor states. The purpose behind such attacks could be an attempt to influence U.S. policy by isolated attacks; foreign espionage agents seeking to exploit information for economic, political, or military intelligence purposes; the application of tactical countermeasures intended to disrupt a specific military weapon or command system; or an attempt to render a major catastrophic blow to the United States by crippling the National Information Infrastructure.

- It is necessary to distinguish between what a layperson might consider a major disruption, such as the three New York airports simultaneously being inoperable for hours, and a strategic impact in which both the scope and duration are of dramatically broader disruptions. The latter is likely to occur at a time in which other contemporaneous events make the impact potentially strategic, such as during a major force deployment.

The task force struggled with the issue of what would truly constitute a strategic attack or strategic impact on the United States. The old paradigms of "n" nuclear weapons, or threats to overthrow the United States per se, were marginally helpful in understanding the degree to which we are vulnerable today to information warfare attack in all of its dimensions. Couple this issue with the difficulty in assessing the real impact of cascading effects through the infrastructures: on the one hand, as being major nuisances and inconveniences to our way of life, or on the other hand, as literally threatening the existence of the United States itself, or threatening the ability of the United States to mount its defenses.

The task force concluded that, in this new world, an event or series of events would be considered strategic either because the impact was so broad and pervasive or because the events occurred at times and places that affected (or could affect) our ability to conduct our necessary affairs. One example we used to illustrate this latter point was a disruption in the area phone, power, and transportation systems coincident with our attempts to embark and move major military forces through that area to points abroad.

What does this mean to nonmilitary organizations? Simple. The threat posed by information warfare is not limited to the realm of national defense, and the effort to control the problem must encompass broader national security interests, including Congress, the civil agencies, regulatory bodies, law enforcement, the intelligence community, and the private sector.

Unlike an attacker in conventional war, an attacker using the tools of information warfare can strike at critical civil functions and processes, such as telecommunications, electric power, banking, or transportation and other centers of gravity or even at the stability of the social structure, without first engaging the military. Such a strategic information warfare attack can occur without forewarning or escalation of other events. In addition, attacks on the civil infrastructure could impede the actions of the military as much as a direct attack on the military's force generation processes or command and control.

Also keep in mind that information warfare is not limited to attacks on computers: The potential targets of information warfare attacks can include information, information systems, people, and facilities that support critical information-dependent functions. The means of attack can be both cyber and physical. Finally, information warfare is adaptive, and the practitioners learn from their experiences. Although this phenomenon is not unique to information warfare, the speed at which the learning process takes place has no parallel in other forms of warfare.

How the threat of information warfare could affect the day-to-day functioning of a country is illustrated in the weaknesses in Supervisory Control and

Data Acquisition (SCADA) systems. In 2003 the House Subcommittee on Technology, Information Policy, Intergovernmental Relations and the Census held a hearing on the security of SCADA systems. These systems are used to manage infrastructure such as the electric power grid and oil and gas pipelines. Senator Adam Putnam, chair of the subcommittee, said the lack of a national strategy to deal with SCADA system security makes the nation undeniably vulnerable to cyberterrorism.

James McDonnell, director of the Protective Security Division at the Department of Homeland Security (DHS), told Putnam and other lawmakers that it is his job to coordinate both physical and cybersecurity for more than 1,700 facilities identified so far as containing critical national security infrastructure systems. Of those facilities, 565 contain SCADA systems that must be protected. McDonnell outlined a series of physical security efforts, such as site security assessments and buffer zone protection mechanisms, underlying the DHS's existing strategy for SCADA security.

According to McDonnell, the National Communications System (NCS) is working with the Idaho National Engineering and Environmental Lab to conduct communications modeling and simulation of SCADA systems, known as the National SCADA Test Bed. The NCS has initiated a study of vulnerabilities in the natural gas pipeline system throughout the eastern United States. Other efforts are underway to identify the high-power microwave vulnerabilities of commercial SCADA systems.

The General Accounting Office (GAO) also released a detailed study of SCADA system security.[2] In its report, the GAO concluded that the DHS has not moved as fast as it could to work with the private sector to improve SCADA security. One big concern identified by the GAO is that it may not be economically feasible for many utilities and other companies that operate critical infrastructure to undertake security upgrades on their own. In addition, Robert Dacey, the GAO's director of information security issues and the primary author of the study, said that software suppliers that develop applications for use on SCADA systems are not promoting security because they do not think companies want to spend the money needed. Several suppliers suggested that because there have been no reports of significant disruptions caused by cyberattacks on control systems, industry representatives believe the threat of such an attack is low, according to Dacey.

This has led to the absence of a formal process of collecting incident data on SCADA systems, further contributing to the skepticism of control systems suppliers. Gerald Freese, director of information security at American Electric Power, said SCADA systems remain open books to any terrorist organization that wants to learn how to exploit them. In fact, energy companies in the United States assisted Pakistan in developing that country's SCADA and supporting telecommunications infrastructure. Modeling the Pakistani electric power infrastructure on the United States, these companies used many of the same technologies and many of the same suppliers to do the work.

Richard Clarke and Howard Schmidt, the two former chairpersons of the President's Critical Infrastructure Protection Board, acknowledged in interviews that raids conducted during the war on terrorism have uncovered evidence that al-Qaeda has been actively studying vulnerabilities in U.S. SCADA systems. Experts in control systems have verified numerous incidents that have affected control systems. Reported attacks include the following:

- In 1994, the computer system of the Salt River Project, a major water and electricity provider in Phoenix, Arizona, was breached.

- In the spring of 2000, a former employee of an Australian company that develops manufacturing software applied for a job with the local government, but was rejected. Over a two-month period, the disgruntled rejected employee reportedly used a radio transmitter on as many as 46 occasions to remotely hack into the controls of a sewage treatment system and ultimately release about 264,000 gallons of raw sewage into nearby rivers and parks.

- In the spring of 2001, hackers mounted an attack on systems that were part of a development network at the California Independent System Operator, a facility that is integral to the movement of electricity throughout the state.

- In August 2003, the Nuclear Regulatory Commission confirmed that in January 2003, the Microsoft SQL Server worm—otherwise known as Slammer—infected a private computer network at the Davis-Besse nuclear power plant in Oak Harbor, Ohio, disabling a safety monitoring system for nearly 5 hours. In addition, the plant's process computer failed, and it took about 6 hours for it to become available again. Slammer reportedly also affected communications on the control networks of at least five other utilities by propagating so quickly that control system traffic was blocked.

Where does all of this leave the average nonmilitary IT security personnel and the managers of the organizations for which they work? Potentially in the crossfire. This is true for many reasons. First, if large-scale information warfare becomes a reality, you can pretty much forget about Internet access for days at a time. Second, as if there is anything worse, if your systems are compromised and used for attack purposes, a SWAT team could break down your doors while they point guns at your employees and yell at them to get on the floor. Third, and perhaps more severe, the SWAT team walks out with all of your computers. The next time you see those computers could be while you and all of your employees are standing in the unemployment line.

Will military-style information warfare happen? People like to have wars, so the answer is that probably someday it will happen. It will be better for any organization that depends on its computers to have reasonable security in place to make sure that the systems are not easily compromised. Thus the SWAT team will not show up at the door, and when Internet communications are restored, you can go on about your business.

OPEN-SOURCE INFORMATION WARFARE

The concept of open-source information warfare is a relatively new aspect of information warfare. The central theme of open-source information warfare is that small, coordinated groups of attackers can use the same tools and tactics that sophisticated military units have been trained in to attack cyberinfrastructures to disrupt commercial and government operations. This includes the widespread use of malicious code attacks.

The FBI fears this type of attack, as do other government agencies charged with maintaining cyber law and order. The potential damage to U.S. national security from a cyber-based attack includes devastating interruptions of critical communications, transportation, and other services. Additionally, such attacks could be used to access and steal protected information and plans.

Military-style information warfare and cyberterrorism were compared in an October 17, 2003, Congressional Research Service study entitled *Computer Attack and Cyber Terrorism: Vulnerabilities and Policy Issues for Congress*, authored by Clay Wilson, Specialist in Technology and National Security, Foreign Affairs, Defense, and Trade Division. The study pointed out that many Pentagon officials reportedly believe that future adversaries may be unwilling to array conventional forces against the United States, and instead may resort to asymmetric warfare, where a less powerful opponent uses other strategies to off-set and negate its adversary's technologic superiority. Also, partly because the military relies significantly on the civilian information infrastructure, these officials believe that future conflicts may be characterized by a blurring in distinction between civilian and military targets. As a consequence, they believe that government and civilian computers and information systems are increasingly becoming a viable target for opponents of the United States.

The study noted that several simulations have been conducted to determine the effects that a cyberattack might have on the defenses and critical infrastructure of the United States. In these tests, it was determined that greater coordination among agencies as well as improved skills on the part of defenders would be necessary to defend against an actual attack. The mock attacks and simulations included the following:

- In 1997, the DoD conducted a mock cyberattack, Eligible Receiver 1997, to test the ability of DOD systems to respond to protect the national information infrastructure.

- In October 2002, Eligible Receiver 2003 was conducted as a follow-up to the 1997 mock attack to determine if efforts to improve security were successful.

- In July 2002, the Naval War College hosted a three-day war game called Digital Pearl Harbor in order to help develop a scenario for coordinated, cross-industry simulations of state-sponsored cyberwarfare attacks.

In the United States, the FBI is the lead law enforcement agency for investigating cyberattacks by foreign adversaries and terrorists. The Cyber Division of the FBI coordinates, supervises, and facilitates prosecution of federal violations in which the Internet, computer systems, or networks are exploited as the principal instruments or targets of terrorist organizations or foreign government–sponsored intelligence operations.

James E. Farnan, Deputy Assistant Director, Cyber Division of the FBI, testified before the House Financial Services Committee, Subcommittee on Financial Institutions and Consumer Credit, and Oversight and Investigations on April 3, 2003. He stated that the cyberthreat to the United States is rapidly expanding, as the number of actors with the ability to utilize computers for illegal, harmful, and possibly devastating purposes is on the rise.

Farnan reported that the Cyber Division is taking a two-track approach toward protecting cyberspace. One avenue is identified as traditional criminal activity that has migrated to the Internet, such as Internet fraud, online identity theft, Internet child pornography, theft of trade secrets, and other similar crimes. The other, nontraditional approach consists of Internet-facilitated activity that did not exist before the establishment of computers, networks, and the World Wide Web. This encompasses cyberterrorism, terrorist threats, foreign intelligence operations, and criminal activity precipitated by illegal computer intrusions into computer networks, including the disruption of computer-supported operations and the theft of sensitive data via the Internet.

In testimony before the House Committee on Government Reform on May 15, 2003, Farnan reported that many computer intrusions are never reported because companies fear a loss of business from reduced consumer confidence in their security measures or from a fear of lawsuits. Most of the outsider-intrusions cases opened during the last few years are the result of a failure to patch a known vulnerability for which a patch has been issued.

Farnan asserted that the FBI has seen a steady increase in computer intrusion/hacking cases. With the proliferation of turnkey hacking tools/utilities available on the Internet, this trend is not surprising. Turnkey tools require no special knowledge to apply the tool: you only need to download the tool and use it. In many cases, computer intrusion incidents may represent the front end of a criminal matter, where credit card fraud, economic espionage, and/or identity theft represent the final result and the intended purpose of the scheme. In some cases, a computer intrusion may also have been for the purpose of installing a Trojan or backdoor that the hacker can later access. The hacker may want to launch a denial-of-service attack or to access financial or other sensitive data contained on that system.

Farnan also reported that the FBI has seen an increasing number of instances where victims have determined that a Trojan/backdoor was installed on their computers during a download from a peer-to-peer (P2P) network. In some cases, the victims also learned that personal and financial information had also been removed from their computers via the backdoor. In addition to traditional Trojans/ backdoors, The FBI has seen an increase in matters where certain bots (active Trojans) have been installed inadvertently via a P2P download. In these instances, the victim computer, via the bot, essentially reports to a designated Internet relay chat (IRC) site, awaiting further instructions from its creator. The creator of the bot will often use the compromised computers to launch coordinated denial-of-service attacks against a targeted site or sites. These bots could also be used to retrieve sensitive information from victim computers in furtherance of an identity theft scheme.

A person using P2P utilities for unauthorized or illegal purposes is not as likely to tell the FBI that an exploit (backdoor) was found on his or her system, or that as a result, certain personal or financial information may have been taken. The FBI has been made aware of instances where Trojans or bots have been found on computer systems where P2P programs are present, and where certain personal, financial, or other sensitive information has been taken.

On September 4, 2003, Larry A. Mefford, Executive Assistant Director of the FBI, testified before the Subcommittee on Cybersecurity, Science, and Research and Development, and the Subcommittee on Infrastructure and Border Security of the Select Committee on Homeland Security. He reported that the FBI, in cooperation with the Department of Energy (DoE), the Department of Homeland Security (DHS), the North American Electrical Reliability Council (NERC), and Canadian authorities aggressively investigated the August 14, 2003 power outages. He stated that to date they have not discovered any evidence indicating that the outages were the result of activity by international or domestic terrorists or other criminal activity. He said that the FBI remains very alert, however, to the possibility that terrorists may target the electrical power grid and other infrastructure facilities. They are clearly aware of the importance of electrical power to the national economy and livelihood. Al-Qaeda and other terrorist groups are known to have considered energy facilities and other infrastructure facilities as possible targets.

In addition, guerillas and extremist groups around the world have attacked power lines as standard targets. Domestic extremists have also targeted energy facilities. In 1986, the FBI disrupted a plan by a radical splinter element of an environmental group to attack power plants in Arizona, California, and Colorado. Terrorists would choose a variety of means to attack the electrical power grids, ranging from blowing up power wire pylons to major attacks against conventional or nuclear power plants.

Mefford contended that the Patriot Act had enhanced the FBI's ability to disrupt terrorist plots. The provisions of the Patriot Act allowing the freer flow of information between intelligence and law enforcement are essential to uncovering and foiling terrorist plots, and they have allowed the FBI to fuse law enforcement and intelligence missions to enhance our preventive capabilities. Given the potential to disrupt critical infrastructure via computer intrusion, the provision of the Patriot Act that allows law enforcement, with the permission of the system owner, to monitor computer trespassers is of particular note. This provision puts cyberintruders on the same footing as physical intruders and means that hacking victims can seek law enforcement assistance in much the same way as burglary victims can invite police officers into their homes to monitor and catch burglars.

On February 24, 2004, Keith Lourdeau, Deputy Assistant Director, Cyber Division of the FBI, testified before the Senate Judiciary Subcommittee on Terrorism, Technology, and Homeland Security. He asserted that as the Internet becomes an increasingly more integral part of our society, new digital vulnerabilities make networked systems potential targets to an increasing number of individuals, including terrorists. To address this threat, protecting the United States from terrorist attack has become the number-one priority of the FBI, and the Cyber Division's number-one priority is designated counterterrorism-related computer intrusions.

He stated that networked systems make inviting targets for terrorists because of the potential for large-scale impact to the nation. The vulnerabilities to networked systems arise from several sources, such as easy accessibility to those systems via the Internet and the harmful tools that are widely available to anyone with a point-and-click ability. Furthermore, the globalization of our nation's infrastructures increases their exposure to potential harm, and the interdependencies of networked systems make attack consequences more difficult to predict and perhaps more severe.

He also emphasized that it is crucial to understand the interrelationship between physical and cybersecurity in the current technological environment. Coordinated attacks on multiple regions could achieve a national effect. The true threat of cyberterrorism will be realized when all of the factors that constitute a terrorist attack, coupled with the use of the Internet, are met.

Lourdeau reiterated the position that the cyberterrorism threat to the United States is rapidly expanding, as the number of actors with the ability to utilize computers for illegal, harmful, and possibly devastating purposes is on the rise. Terrorist groups have shown a clear interest in developing basic hacking tools, and the FBI predicts that terrorist groups will either develop or hire hackers, particularly to complement large physical attacks with cyberattacks.

If a terrorist lacked the technical sophistication to conduct a computer attack and chose to recruit a hacker, potential damage would be increased if that hacker was an insider. Insider attacks originate from a variety of motivations (e.g., financial gain, personal grievances, revenge, recruitment, or coercion). It is not necessarily the motivation that makes insiders dangerous, but the fact that they may have unfiltered access to sensitive computer systems that can place public safety at risk. Moreover, there is an increasing concern over the prevalent trend to outsource, even to foreign conglomerates, for services that were previously handled domestically.

Attacks against regional targets could have a significant effect on computer networks, while coordinated attacks on multiple regions could achieve a national effect with severe repercussions. There are numerous control systems whose destruction would have a far-reaching effect. Large-scale distribution systems, such as those involving natural gas, oil, electric power, and water, tend to use automated SCADA systems for administration. SCADA systems tend to have both cyber and physical vulnerabilities. Poor computer security, lack of encryption, and poor enforcement of user privileges lead to risks to SCADA systems. Poor physical controls can make the disruption of the SCADA system a realistic possibility.

A major method used in preventing cyberterrorism is the sharing of intelligence information. The FBI routinely passes intelligence received in active investigations or developed through research to the intelligence community. Throughout the FBI field offices, Special Agents serve on cyber task forces with other agencies. The FBI is a sponsor/participant in the Interagency Coordination Cell (IACC) at FBI headquarters. This environment of information sharing and cooperation is expanding to include foreign governments such as the "5 Eyes."

Cyber programs are unique in nature. However, taking proactive investigative measures with tools such as honey pots/nets and undercover operations enhances the FBI's ability to prevent a cyberterrorist attack. The FBI has undertaken the following initiatives to combat cyberterrorism:

- Cyber task forces
- Public–Private alliances
- International cyber investigative support
- Mobile cyber assistance teams

- Cyber action teams
- Cyber investigators training
- A cyber intelligence center
- Cyber tactical analytical case support

The Computer Intrusion program provides administrative and operational support and guidance to the field offices investigating computer intrusions, assists other FBI programs that have a computer dimension, and coordinates computer intrusion investigations by various criminal investigative and intelligence components of the federal government. The Special Technologies and Applications program supports FBI counterterrorism computer intrusion–related investigations with all necessary equipment and technical investigative tools.

The Cyber International Investigative program creates the ability to conduct international cyber investigative efforts through coordination with the FBI Headquarters Office of International Operations, legal attache offices, and foreign law enforcement agencies.

The Cyber Specialized Training program coordinates with the Engineering Research Facility, Laboratory Division, Training Division, National White Collar Crime Center, private industry, academia, and others to deliver training to FBI cybersquads, task forces, international law enforcement officers, and others.

In the event of a cyberterrorist attack, the FBI will conduct an intense postincident investigation to determine the source, including the motive and purpose of the attack. In the digital age, data collection in that investigation can be extremely difficult. The computer industry is also conducting research and development involving basic security, such as developing cryptographic hardware that will filter attempts to introduce malicious code or stop unauthorized activity. The following incidents are an indication of the ability of individuals to gain access to our networked systems and the possible damage that can result:

- In 1996, an individual used simple explosive devices to destroy the master terminal of a hydroelectric dam in Oregon. Although there was no effect on the dam's structure, this simple attack completely disabled the dam's power-generating turbines and forced a switch to manual control. A coordinated attack on a region's infrastructure systems (e.g., the SCADA systems that control Washington D.C.'s electric power, natural gas, and water supply) would have a profound effect on the nation's sense of security. This incident demonstrated how minimal sophistication and material can destroy a SCADA system.

- In 1997, a juvenile accessed the Generation Digital Loop Carrier System operated by NYNEX. Several commands were sent that disrupted the telephone service to the Federal Aviation Administration (FAA) tower at the Worcester Airport, to the Worcester Airport Fire Department, and to other related entities such as airport security, the weather service, and various private airfreight companies. As a result of this disruption, the main radio transmitter and the circuit that enabled aircraft to send an electronic signal to activate the runway lights on approach were disabled. This same individual then accessed the loop carrier system for customers in and around Rutland, Massachusetts, and sent commands that disabled the telephone service, including the 911 service, throughout the Rutland area.

- On May 3, 2003, an e-mail was sent to the National Science Foundation's (NSF) Network Operations Center that read, "I've hacked into the server of your South Pole Research Station. Pay me off, or I will sell the station's data to another country and tell the world how vulnerable you are." The e-mail contained data found only on the NSF's computer systems, proving that this was no hoax. NSF personnel immediately shut down the penetrated servers. During May, the temperature at the South Pole can get down to 70 degrees below zero Fahrenheit; aircraft cannot land there until November because of the harsh weather conditions. The compromised computer systems controlled the life support systems for the 50 scientists wintering at the South Pole Station.

Lourdeau further testified that the unique complexity of protecting our nation's networked systems is a daunting task. The key to prevention is effective attack warning and the education of the owners and operators of those systems. The protection of our networked systems is a shared responsibility and partnership between the private sector, state and local law enforcement agencies, federal law enforcement agencies, the DHS, and the intelligence community, both domestic and foreign. The FBI encourages international cooperation to help manage this increasingly global problem.

In addition, Lourdeau stated that defending against a cyberattack requires the integration of operational, physical, communication, and personnel security measures. This involves a full range of matters such as installing effective passwords and firewall protection, avoidance of unprotected and unnecessarily opened entry points, installation of default configuration and passwords, minimization of placing servers in unprotected areas, and vigilance against disgruntled employees.

MILITANCY AND SOCIAL ACTION

As if facing the potential of military-style information warfare or open-source information warfare is not bad enough, there is also an increasing frequency of militancy, social, action, and political protests occurring on the Internet. Many people refer to this as *hactivism*. One high-profile example of hactivism occurred in December 1999, as the World Trade Organization (WTO) held a summit in Seattle, Washington, and many political activists protested in the street. Meanwhile, a group calling themselves the Electrohippies, which is a U.K.-based electronic activism and civil disobedience group, was active on the Internet, hitting the WTO website with a denial-of-service attack.

In October of 2001, the National Infrastructure Protection Center released a report entitled *Cyber Protests: The Threat to the U.S. Information Infrastructure*, which illustrated how events like the 1999 WTO summit was prompting militancy on the Internet. The report asserted that as computing technology becomes faster and better and hacking tools become more advanced and easier to use, cyberprotesting and hactivism will become more significant to U.S. national interests.

The report asserted that cyberprotesters were becoming increasingly more organized and their techniques more sophisticated. It was expected that there would be an increase in the number of apparently unrelated hacking groups participating in the cyberprotests. National boundaries will not always be clearly delineated in attacks on opposing organizations. International activity will also tend to spill over into the United States. Because the United States is a multicultural, world-leading nation, it will suffer from attacks on culturally related sites and structures in the future.

The case studies in the report showed that most popularly targeted sites are those belonging to government, educational, commercial, and cultural institutions. However, any site with an exploitable vulnerability will be susceptible to a cyberattack. The infrastructure has been targeted in other countries in cyber-protests, and it is expected that it will eventually be targeted in the United States as well. Cyberprotesters certainly will target infrastructure more often and exploit opportunities to disrupt or damage it.

Web sites that remain open to known hacking tools will have a higher probability of suffering defacement. Network administrators must remain educated, and defenses must evolve along with the threats and offensive capabilities. Although the cyberprotests seen today have already caused limited damage, the potential for future attacks could bring about large economic losses as well as potentially severe damage to the national infrastructure, affecting global markets as well as public safety.

Cyberprotesters have a wide range of goals or objectives. Some hackers want to expose government corruption or fundamental violations of human rights, whereas others just want to hack and cause mischief for fun. The most common type of cyberprotest comes in the form of Web page defacements. In such scenarios, a Web site is compromised through some security deficiency, and the hacker is able to alter it, often placing propaganda, profanity, or pornographic images on it. This can range from being a nuisance and embarrassment for an organization to a major economic loss for an e-commerce business.

Another high-profile incident occurred in May 1999 after the United States bombed the Chinese embassy in Belgrade, Yugoslavia, during the NATO air campaign. U.S. Web sites were defaced in the name of China, and massive e-mail campaigns were executed to gain sympathy and support for the Chinese cause. Government Web sites were primarily targeted. The U.S. Departments of Energy and the Interior and the National Park Service all suffered Web page defacements. In addition, the White House Web site was taken down for three days after it was continually mail bombed. This action was relatively unorganized in fashion, short in length, and affected a small number of Web sites in the United States.

Pro-Chinese hackers also acted against Taiwan during the Taiwanese presidential elections in August and September 1999. Cyberprotesters and hactivists compromised 165 Taiwanese Web sites, mainly defacing them, over the two-month period. Their ultimate goal, as it was stated, was to negatively affect and bring down Taiwan's infrastructure. Among the targeted sites were electricity, economic institutions, telecommunications, and air traffic control.

In late April and early May 2001, pro-Chinese hactivists and cyberprotesters began a cyber assault on U.S. Web sites. This action resulted from an incident in early April when a Chinese fighter jet was lost at sea after colliding with a U.S. naval reconnaissance airplane. It also coincided with the two-year anniversary of the Chinese embassy bombing by the United States in Belgrade and the traditionally celebrated May Day and Youth Day in China. Led by the Honkers Union of China (HUC), pro-Chinese hackers defaced or crashed more than 100 seemingly random Web sites, mainly .gov and .com, through denial-of-service attacks and similar exploits. Many defacements of Web sites included posting pictures of the dead Chinese pilot Wang Wei and profane messages calling for the downfall of the United States. Pro-U.S. hackers responded with similar defacements, messages, and damage on 300 Chinese Web sites.

In October 2000, Israeli and Palestinian hackers engaged in adversarial hacking when the prolonged peace talks between the two groups broke down. During this difficult time, hackers seized the opportunity to attack Web sites belonging to the opposition. Starting on October 6, 2000, 40 Israeli Web sites and at least 15 Palestinian Web sites suffered defacements at the hands of opposing hackers.

These events attracted a wide variety of hackers eager to join the fight. Both sides were well-organized and used reconnaissance and intelligence-gathering techniques to maximize their effectiveness. Even outside hacking groups, such as G-Force Pakistan, joined forces with the Palestinians to lend a helping hand. This is increasingly common. Some outside groups join an effort because they have similar political or ethnic motivations, but this is not always the case. Some groups participate in hacks simply for the desire to hack or the publicity, not out of a sense of loyalty.

Overall, it can be expected that Israeli and Palestinian hackers will be active whenever a stumbling block appears in the road to possible peace between the groups. On the other hand, increased hacking might also occur when the Israelis and Palestinians are close to a peace agreement. System administrators must remain vigilant and focused on providing effective network security. Another example is India and Pakistan engaging in cyberprotest caused by national and ethnic differences. After a cease-fire in the Kashmir Valley, hackers took it upon themselves to continue the hostilities. In 2000, pro-Pakistani hackers defaced more than 500 Indian Web sites. Conversely, only one known Pakistani site was hacked by the Indians. The group G-Force Pakistan was the most active group claiming involvement in the events.

Japan has been targeted twice in online protests. During the first week of April 2001, pro-Korean hackers attacked Japanese organizations responsible for the approval of a new history textbook. The textbook glossed over atrocities committed by Japan during World War II and the occupation of China and South Korea. The perceived reluctance of Japan to accept responsibility for its actions triggered these events. The main participants in this incident were Korean university students, who used e-mail bombs in a denial-of-service attack. The students crashed several Web sites, including Japan's Education Ministry, Liberal Democratic Party, and the publishing company responsible for the textbook. These attacks were neither long-lasting nor largely organized.

In early August 2001, pro-Chinese hackers targeted Japanese Web sites after Japan's Prime Minister visited a controversial war memorial, the Yasukuni Shrine. In a brief period of time, hackers defaced several Web sites belonging mainly to Japanese companies and research institutes.

In March 2003, the FBI investigated the defacement of an al-Jazeera Web site after unidentified hackers replaced the Qatari news outlet's site with a stars-and-stripes logo. The Arabic and English versions of the popular television channel were down for at least 24 hours.

HOMELAND SECURITY EFFORTS

The FBI and the United States Secret Service both have troops on the frontlines of cyberspace. The efforts of these two organizations in addressing cybercrime and cyberterrorism are respected around the world.

InfraGard is a partnership between private industry and the U.S. government (represented by the FBI). The InfraGard initiative was developed to encourage the exchange of information by the government and the private-sector members. Private-sector members and an FBI field representative form local area chapters. These chapters set up their own boards to govern and share information within the membership. The FBI plays the part of facilitator by doing the following:

- Gathering information and distributing it to members
- Educating the public and members on infrastructure protection
- Disseminating information through the InfraGard network

- Producing valuable analytic products on information received through the InfraGard network

- Opening the doors of communication between government and private-sector members

The National InfraGard Program began as a pilot project in 1996, when the Cleveland FBI field office asked local computer professionals to assist the FBI in determining how to better protect critical information systems in the public and private sectors. From this new partnership, the first InfraGard chapter was formed to address both cyber and physical threats.

The FBI, in conjunction with representatives from private industry, the academic community, and the public sector, further developed the InfraGard initiative to expand direct contacts with the private-sector infrastructure owners and operators and to share information about cyber intrusions, exploited vulnerabilities, and infrastructure threats. The initiative, encouraging the exchange of information by government and private-sector members, continued to expand through the formation of additional InfraGard chapters, within the jurisdiction of each FBI field office. InfraGard Secure Access Members can report incidents through the secure Web site using the online report in the incident reports area. Members may also report through the following mechanisms:

- Contacting the Watch and Warning Unit at 202-323-3205

- Contacting the local InfraGard Coordinator

- Faxing incident reports via unsecure fax to the Watch and Warning Unit at 202-323-2079 or 202-323-2082

- E-mailing reports to the Watch and Warning Unit using secure e-mail to infragard-hq@fbi.gov

The FBI public Web site has an online incident reporting form. This form may be used by anyone who wishes to report an incident to the FBI. The information is then verified and sanitized so it can be passed to InfraGard secure members in the form of analytic products or threat assessments. InfraGard members are bound by a code of ethics to do the following:

- Promote the protection and advancement of the critical infrastructure of the United States of America.

- Cooperate with others in the interchange of knowledge and ideas for mutual protection.

- Support the education of members and the general public in a diligent, loyal, and honest manner, and not knowingly be a part of any illegal or improper activities.

- Serve in the interests of InfraGard and the general public in a diligent, loyal, and honest manner, and not knowingly be a party to any illegal or improper activities.

- Abide by the National and Local Chapter InfraGard Bylaws.

- Protect and respect the privacy rights, civil rights, and physical and intellectual property rights of others.

- Maintain confidentiality, and prevent the use for competitive advantage at the expense of other members, of information obtained in the course of involvement with InfraGard, which includes but is not limited to information concerning the business of a fellow member or company, information identified as proprietary, confidential, or sensitive.

The United States Secret Service has also had a role in fighting cybercrime and terrorism. Since its inception in 1865, it has grown from its initial mandate to suppress the counterfeiting of currency to protecting the integrity of the nation's financial payment systems. During this time, modes and methods of payment have evolved, and so has the Secret Service mission. Computers and other chip-based devices are now the facilitators of criminal activity or the target of such, compelling the involvement of the Secret Service in combating cybercrime. The perpetrators involved in the exploitation of such technology range from traditional fraud artists to violent criminals who recognize new opportunities to expand and diversify their criminal portfolio.

With the exponential growth of emerging technology throughout the world, it only follows that the criminal element will attempt to capitalize on use of this technology to further its quest for anonymity and profitability. In order for law enforcement to remain ahead of the power curve, it must adapt to the changes presented by both technology and criminals in a timely manner. The Secret Service developed a plan of action to achieve this goal by recognizing the need for change and innovative ideas to fight the war on criminal activity through the utilization of nontraditional task forces.

The concept of task forces has been around for many years and has proven to be successful. However, traditional task forces have consisted primarily of law enforcement personnel to the exclusion of other parties that could make significant contributions. The Secret Service developed a new approach to increase the resources, skills, and vision by having local, state, and federal law enforcement team up with prosecutors, private industry, and academia to fully maximize what each has to offer in an effort to combat criminal activity. By forging new relationships with private-sector entities and scholars, the task force opens itself up to a wealth of information and communication lines with limitless potential. The New York Electronic Crimes Task Force (NYECTF) was formed based on this concept and has been highly successful since its inception in 1995.

On October 26, 2001, President Bush signed into law H.R. 3162, the *Uniting and Strengthening America by Providing Appropriate Tools Required to Intercept and Obstruct Terrorism (USA PATRIOT) Act of 2001.* In drafting this particular legislation, Congress recognized the Secret Service philosophy that our success resides in the ability to bring academia, law enforcement, and private industry together to combat crime in the information age. As a result, the U.S. Secret Service was mandated by this Act to establish a nationwide network of Electronic Crimes Task Forces based on the New York model that encompasses this philosophy.

The Electronic Crimes Task Force has grown from a few dedicated individuals to a group of hundreds of industry as well as local, state, and federal law enforcement members throughout the country. At a recent meeting in New York, more than 500 members were in attendance. Many new regional task forces are now being formed throughout the country, and hundreds (soon to be thousands) of law enforcement, government, and industry technology specialists are now networking to help prevent and, when necessary, prosecute these new kinds of crimes. Contact information for these new regional task force locations is listed as follows:

BOSTON

Title: New England Electronic Crimes Task Force

Address: Tip O'Neil Federal Building

10 Causeway Street, Room 791
Boston, MA 02222
Phone: 617-565-6640
Fax: 617-565-5659

CHARLOTTE

Title: Metro-Charlotte Electronic-Financial Crimes Task Force
Address: One Fairview Center
6302 Fairview Road
Charlotte, NC 28210
Phone: 704-442-8370
Fax: 704-442-8369

CHICAGO

Title: Chicago Electronic Crimes Task Force (CECTF)
Address: 525 West Van Buren
Chicago, IL 60607
Phone: 312-353-5431
Fax: 312-353-1225

CLEVELAND

Title: Cleveland Electronic Crimes Task Force
Address: 6100 Rockside Woods Blvd.
Cleveland, OH 44131-2334
Phone: 216-706-4365
Fax: 216-706-4445

DALLAS

Title: Dallas N-Tec Electronic Crimes Task Force
Address: 125 East John W. Carpenter

Irvine, TX 75062-2752

Phone: 972-868-3200

HOUSTON

Title: Houston HITEC Electronic Crimes Task Force

Address: 602 Sawyer Street

Houston, TX 77007

Phone: 713-868-2299

Fax: 713-868-5093

LAS VEGAS

Title: Las Vegas Electronic Crimes Task Force

Address: 600 Las Vegas Blvd. South, Suite 700

Las Vegas, NV 89101

Phone: 702-388-6571

Fax: 702-388-6668

LOS ANGELES

Title: Los Angeles Electronic Crimes Task Force

Address: 725 South Figueroa Street, 13th Floor

Los Angeles, CA 90017-5418

Phone: 213-894-4830 (General Office for USSS)

Phone: 213-533-4650 (Direct Phone for ECTF)

MIAMI

Title: Miami Electronic Crimes Task Force

Address: 8375 NW 53rd Street

Miami, FL 33166

Phone: 305-629-1800

Fax: 305-629-1830

NEW YORK

Title: New York Electronic Crimes Task Force

Address: 335 Adams Street, 32nd Floor

Brooklyn, NY 11201

Phone: 718-625-7135

Fax: 718-625-3919

SAN FRANCISCO

Title: Bay Area Electronic Crimes Task Force

Address: 345 Spear Street

San Francisco, CA 94105

Phone: 415-744-9026

Fax: 415-744-9051

SOUTH CAROLINA

Title: South Carolina Electronic Crimes Task Force

Address: 107 Westpark Boulevard, Suite 301

Columbia, SC 29210

Phone: 803-772-4015

WASHINGTON, DC

Title: Washington-Metro Electronic Crimes Task Force

Address: 1100 L Street NW

Washington, DC 20003

Phone: 202-406-8000

Fax: 202-406-8803

ACTION STEPS TO COMBAT MALICIOUS CODE ATTACKS

Organizations can take several steps to help reduce the impact of malicious code attacks. Recommended steps are included at the end of each chapter. The action steps listed in Table 9.1 are designed to help an organization better plan its future IT security efforts.

Action Steps to Combat Malicious Code Attacks

Number	Action Step
9.1	Assess your organization's enemies lists to determine what types of groups may specifically target your computers or networks.
9.2	Evaluate the activities of InfraGard in the cities where your organization has facilities to determine if participation would be beneficial.
9.3	Evaluate the activities of the Electronic Crimes Task Force in the cities where your organization has facilities to determine if participation would be beneficial.
9.4	Evaluate the long-term technology strategies of your organization to determine if they are designed to prepare for future attacks.
9.5	Convene the malicious code work group to examine the results of these evaluations and formulate recommendations for action.

REFERENCES

1. The Report of the Defense Science Board Task Force on Information Warfare - Defense (IW-D), 1996.

2. *Critical Infrastructure Protection: Challenges and Efforts to Secure Control Systems*, United States General Accounting Office, June 2000.

Appendix
Computer Security Resources

CENTRAL COMMAND

www.centralcommand.com/index.html
Virus information for corporate and home users

CERT/CC

www.cert.org/nav/index_main.html
Unit of the Software Engineering Institute (SEI), a federally funded research and development center at Carnegie Mellon University in Pittsburgh, that provides vulnerability analysis, incident handling, and information dissemination

CIO SECURITY AND PRIVACY RESEARCH CENTER

www.cio.com/research/security/
Articles, ask the expert, book reviews, and reports

CISSP AND SSCP OPEN STUDY GUIDE

www.cccure.org
Study guides, tips, and resources

COMMON VULNERABILITIES AND EXPOSURES (CVE)

www.cve.mitre.org
List of standardized names for vulnerabilities and other information security exposures

COMPUTER ASSOCIATES VIRUS INFORMATION CENTER

www3.ca.com/threatinfo/default.aspx
Detailed information on the latest viruses, worms, Trojans, and hoaxes

DEPARTMENT OF HOMELAND SECURITY

www.dhs.gov/dhspublic/
Information on computer security and national protection strategies

FEDERAL TRADE COMMISSION

www.ftc.gov/bcp/conline/edcams/infosecurity/index.html
Information on computer security and e-commerce

F-SECURE SECURITY INFORMATION CENTER

www.f-secure.com/virus-info/
News, hoax warnings, screenshots, and bulletins on the new computer viruses

GFI SECURITY LAB

www.gfi.com/security/
Virus threats, security tests, and information about security

ICSA INFORMATION SECURITY MAGAZINE

infosecuritymag.techtarget.com
Online magazine about computer security

INFOSYSSEC

www.infosyssec.com
Security and hacking guides, tutorials, downloads

INFRAGUARD

www.infragard.net

Public–private sector organization to fight cyber and physical threats to critical infrastructures, with 80 local chapters with industry and FBI representatives

INTERNET SECURITY REVIEW MAGAZINE

www.isr.net

Online magazine about computer security

INTERNET STORM CENTER

isc.incidents.org

System that gathers millions of intrusion detection log entries from around the world to find new virus and worm attacks

MCAFEE AVERT VIRUS INFORMATION LIBRARY

vil.nai.com/vil/

Information on viruses, how they infect systems, and how to remove them

MESSAGELABS: CURRENT THREATS

www.messagelabs.com/viruseye/threats/default.asp

Information on e-mail security threats

MICROSOFT SECURITY ADVISOR

www.microsoft.com/security/

Security tools, documentation, tips, and other information regarding security for users, developers, and businesses

NIST COMPUTER SECURITY RESOURCE CLEARINGHOUSE

csrc.ncsl.nist.gov

The NIST Computer Security Division provides information on security, awareness of IT risks, vulnerabilities, and protection requirements

Also see:

NIST VIRUS INFORMATION PAGE

`csrc.nist.gov/virus`

NSA INFORMATION ASSURANCE PROGRAM

`www.nsa.gov/ia/index.cfm`
Information on detecting, reporting, and responding to cyberthreats

PANDA SOFTWARE VIRUS INFO

`www.pandasoftware.com/virus_info/`
Information and resources on viruses

SC INFO SECURITY MAGAZINE

`www.infosecnews.com`
Online magazine about computer security

SECURITY MAGAZINE

`www.secmag.com`
Online magazine about computer security

SECURITYFOCUS

`www.securityfocus.com`
Extensive computer security information

SECURITYGEEKS

`securitygeeks.shmoo.com`
Security, cryptography, and privacy news

SOPHOS VIRUS INFORMATION

`www.sophos.com/virusinfo/`

Analysis, articles, and other computer virus information

SYMANTEC SECURITY RESPONSE

`securityresponse.symantec.com`

Information on virus threats, security advisories, tools, and other security topics

TREND MICRO VIRUS INFORMATION CENTER

`www.trendmicro.com/vinfo/`

News of viruses, an encyclopedia, security alerts, and options to submit suspicious files

VIRUS BULLETIN

`www.virusbtn.com`

Journal on developments in viruses and antivirus products

VIRUSLIST.COM

`www.viruslist.com/eng/index.html`

Encyclopedia covering hoaxes and viruses with descriptions, warnings, and advice

Index